ESSENTIAL SMALL BUSINESS LEADERSHIP SKILLS

DEVELOP YOUR ORGANIZATION AND STRUCTURE, ACHIEVE SMALL BUSINESS GROWTH, AND COMPLETE COMPLEX BUSINESS TASKS

DIANA ARMSTRONG

JAD PUBLISHING LTD

INTRODUCTION

"There's no shortage of remarkable ideas, what's missing is the will to execute them."
    –Seth Godin

R unning a business is no walk in the park. You have to really think if you consider starting a business. Have I the mental fortitude? Am I prepared to put in the hours? Do I want to struggle with customers, suppliers, and personnel?

And this is just in terms of the mental and motivational requirements. Other things that you must consider are whether you understand enough about the business world, about the industry that you plan to leap into. Do you understand the terminology of business? How to strategize? How to manage people? How to manage your finances? In fact, have you got access to finance at all?

So, running a business isn't for everyone. You may even

have been in business for some time but you are still struggling with some of the things I mentioned above. There are many reasons why you may be turning to this book.

You won't be disappointed.

Why the Need for This Book?

I decided to write this book because, during my years in business, I realized the need for it. Meeting people daily who are struggling to make their business work, or listening to the stories of aspiring business owners made me realize that there is vast potential out there, but also great ignorance about business and the potential pitfalls.

This book is aimed at you, whether you're a struggling business owner or manager, a young person considering starting a business, or just anyone who has an idea about a business. The concepts I discuss here are generic, meaning they'll work for you in any business avenue you wish to pursue. I don't discuss specific industries or markets. I do cover a wide range of the most typical issues that everyone encounters when running a business, small or otherwise. These include matters like working with your people and developing them into teams, how to strategize and develop your financial and marketing plans, and also other, "softer" issues like the importance of honesty in business and how to delegate properly. There are also other topics where I provide information for you to get a holistic overview of all the information that you may require when thinking about setting up shop, or perhaps about turning your present business around.

The Benefits of Reading This Book

You will benefit from this book, whether you know nothing about business or you're an MBA graduate. It'll profit you in the following ways:

- You'll gain an understanding of how a business functions as a system of different, interdependent parts.
- You'll get to know the types of information you need to make proper decisions for your business.
- You'll understand the importance of working with people and why it's imperative that you develop your people into a strong, cohesive team.
- You'll be emboldened by the fact that nothing that I present here is rocket science. Everything I talk about can be done by virtually any person. It only takes commitment and dedication.

I did it, and I knew nothing about the business world. So can you.

1

MOTIVATION: THE FIRE OF PASSION

"And the day came when the risk to remain tight in a bud was more painful than the risk it took to blossom."

Wherefrom Art Thou, Oh Greatness?

The Dutch author and motivational speaker, Jeroen de Flander, speaks in his book, *The Art of Performance,* of the three so-called engines of greatness—passion and purpose, deep practice, and persistence. The areas where these three concepts overlap, if you were to draw each in the shape of a Venn diagram, would be "greatness" (de Flander, 2019).

It is especially important to find one's passion and purpose in order to get to greatness. For you, as an entrepreneur, it may be easy. Often, when a business idea hits you, it feels like you're "running on heroin." You get all fired up and ready to do business. However, leading a team also means transmitting that drive to other members of the team. This is not so simple.

And, let's face it—the larger the business, the more difficult it is to get everyone fired up to the same levels of motivation that you may be feeling. After all, many employees may feel that they have no "skin in the game," that there's no added benefit for them to get so excited about. Or, they may feel that what you view as exciting sounds to them a lot like additional work!

This is where your role as a leader kicks in.

But first, it's important to clarify a few concepts.

What is an Entrepreneur?

The difference between an "ordinary" business person and an entrepreneur is generally seen in the context of the type of business idea being pursued. An entrepreneur is someone who first initiates a business idea or concept and then runs with it in the market. Over the long run this may then turn into a "normal" business, but often (mostly) not.

A further distinguishing characteristic may be seen in the realm of *Blue Ocean Strategy*. In their so-titled book, launched in 2006, Professors Kim and Mauborgne speak of creating "uncontested market space." So, one could also say that an entrepreneur is someone who creates new markets by satisfying new buyer demands (that buyers may not even know they have). Kim and Mauborgne called this Blue Ocean Strategy because, in the process of creating uncontested market space, blue ocean strategists operate outside the field of competition. In contrast, red oceans are red because of the blood of competitors feeding on each other.

Creating such a blue ocean is, of course, much easier said than done. While it's not within the scope of this book to discuss it in detail, in essence, what their book is about is creating a shift in buyer value while also keeping price down. This flies in the face of traditional approaches to business strategy that says you can either be the low-cost producer or the differentiator, but not both. Kim and Mauborgne argue that you can, and should, do both to create new buyer value (Kim & Mauborgne, 2015).

Other differences between a business person and an entrepreneur include the following:

- **Purpose:** Most business people are profit-driven and have to accede to the wishes of stakeholders like the board, shareholders, etc. Entrepreneurs, on the other hand, tend to want to make a difference in the world.
- **Risk:** Because entrepreneurs generally tend to do things they like, they're also much less risk-averse than traditional business people. Entrepreneurs tend to be risk-takers, knowing that if they fail they can always start all over again.
- **Employees:** There tends to be a more formal relationship between a business person and their employees than is the case with an entrepreneur. Entrepreneurs tend to surround themselves with like-minded people in their business, often friends and family.
- **Customers:** Although both are strongly customer-focused, an entrepreneur tends to be almost

obsessive about good customer service, knowing that every little sale counts.

- **Competition:** We've already touched on this, but an entrepreneur doesn't tend to go head-to-head with the competition. He/she tries to create uncontested market space. Their biggest competitor is themselves.

- **Time management:** Business people tend to be a bit obsessive about time management, often erring on the side of micro-managing employees. An entrepreneur tends to be a perfectionist about his or her product or service and will take time to make sure it is correct. In the process, they can drive other employees to distraction!

- **Defining success:** Because a business person is mostly extrinsically motivated, they tend to define success by feedback as it comes at them from stakeholders like customers, the board, shareholders, etc. Entrepreneurs tend to be more intrinsically motivated and know when they have done a good job (*10 Differences between a Businessman and Entrepreneur*, 2019).

In the final analysis, though, this isn't a book about the differences between a business person and an entrepreneur. Both need each other. And successful entrepreneurs tend to become business people in their own right, so whatever I suggest here for operating a successful business applies to you whether you see yourself as an entrepreneur or business person. I just wanted to show that there's a "timeline" of development between the two concepts where there may be certain environmental exigencies that may apply more depending on whether you operate as a normal business, or as an entrepreneur.

Both concepts mean you have to know how to deal with customers, you have to know the basics of financial management, and you have to be a great boss! People's motivation is important, whether you consider yourself to be a business person or an entrepreneur. You can only get stuff done through and with your people. If your people aren't engaged, your business cannot prosper.

The Reasons Why it is Important

Research undertaken even before the COVID-19 pandemic showed that 40% of employees were concerned that they could lose their jobs, while 30% of employees were constantly surfing the internet looking for other work (Hassell, n.d.). This is all about employee engagement, or lack thereof. Research undertaken by Gallup shows that the average level of employee engagement worldwide is 22% (*Engage Your Employees to See High Performance and Innovation*, 2021).

One of a leader's most important functions is to ensure employee engagement. The organization cannot advance if the employees are not engaged. So, what's the difference between engaged and non-engaged employees, I hear you ask? Simply this—engaged employees are happy and want to get on with the job, making the most of every day.

Conversely, disengaged employees are unhappy and unmotivated and undermine the efforts of engaged personnel to do the job. They may do this consciously or unconsciously, but either way, they stifle productivity.

A study undertaken by Gallup of 1.8 million employees worldwide confirmed the link between employee engagement and performance outcomes in all of the following areas:

- Absenteeism
- Customer satisfaction
- Patient safety incidents
- Productivity
- Profitability
- Quality (defects)
- Safety incidents
- Shrinkage (theft)
- Turnover (Reilly, 2021)

This makes a strong case for ensuring that your employees are engaged, not forgetting, of course, the motivational imperative! So, how does one go about it?

Getting Engagement

There are several things that you can do:

- **Ask for their views:** A major motivator and a way to obtain employee engagement is to ask them about their viewpoints on matters. People value it when they're asked their opinion on an issue pertaining to the business. It's a very easy method to obtain buy-in, cooperation, and to improve enthusiasm and motivation! Do this, whether it's about a new product, a new procedure, or just a general, "What do you think we can do to improve things around here?" Be careful not to open a pandora's box of complaints though! I always involve some junior people in my strategic planning sessions with a threefold purpose: (a) to make them feel that they're valued, (b) to ensure that they get a feel of how senior management thinks and what we consider to be important drivers in the business environment, and (c) for their education—they will, after all, be the future decision-makers who have to know how to strategize! Importantly though—if juniors in the organization feel that they're valued enough to take part in developing the organization's strategy, it immediately gets their buy-in in implementing the strategy.

- **Set an example:** Whatever your leadership style, you have to set an example. Explain where you're heading and how you'll measure whether the team is successful. You have to define the vision with them and then show that you live the vision, and that you're honest in all your dealings with them (Wheeler & Bhadresa, 2020).

- **Ensure collaboration:** Teamwork is essential for business success and I'll deal with developing teams in more detail later. At this early stage, suffice it to say that you have to provide your team with the infrastructure and tools that will make collaboration easy. So, it's not just about explaining to them how important teamwork is and setting an example. You have to make sure that they have the real and/or remote tools to do the work. As soon as people have to look for workarounds to get stuff done because the tools or infrastructure isn't optimal, productivity will falter.

- **Develop success champions:** The old saying that success breeds success holds true. Teams should share their experiences about what worked and what did not, and the leader should be actively involved in the telling of these stories (Wheeler & Bhadresa, 2020).

- **Make the organization a meritocracy:** People must know that rewards are based on achievements, that mediocrity does not get awarded. Rewards can be person-based, but it's usually better if it's team-based, meaning that the team gets rewarded for a job well done. This has the added advantage that the team will ensure that poor performers are either motivated to do a proper job or that they'll get worked out.

- **Set proper goals for engagement:** People's engagement goals and organizational performance goals should be linked together so that the person can aspire to perform, but at the same time will be supporting the organization's goal achievement. If you separate these goals, it leads to confusion. This should become routine, so that there's virtually no distinction between functional goals and engagement goals because, after all, one significantly influences the other (Reilly, 2014).

- **Find out what motivates them:** Different people are motivated by different things, because we're all different. For some, the best motivator may be time off. For others, maybe more solace when they do the work. For others, it may be the power of verbal rewards, a quick "thank you" now and then. Find out what the correct triggers are for each individual and apply situational leadership.

- **Give feedback:** People want to know what they're doing wrong, but also what they're doing right. It's the fundamental cornerstone of people's motivation at work. And it has to be a continuous process, not relegated to a performance assessment once a year (Clapon, 2017).
- **Develop them:** A 2018 SmartCompany survey revealed that 40% of polled employees wanted to learn more, especially about how to develop a team (Kraus, 2019). People are hungry for knowledge. It's a big incentive if you have a proper people development program in your business that has as its basis both formal and informal training. It may also be worth your while to invest in proper mentoring and coaching programs.
- **Make them feel important:** Employees need to be shown how their outputs contribute to organizational success and vision achievement. Everyone, down to the cleaner, needs to be shown how what they do daily contributes to the bottom line. Using a Balanced Scorecard, which we'll get to later in the book, is a good way to do this.
- **Encourage them to take risks:** People only grow when they move out of their comfort zones. You should encourage your employees to take risks, not in a way that could crash your business, but in a calculated way. All employees should know that the

boss may be approached at any time with suggestions to improve the work, as only one example.

- **Invest in talent management:** Some degree of personnel turnover is healthy for an organization. I can't say what percentage is acceptable, because it will depend on the type of business. Of course, you can't afford to have half your top performers leave the business every year, so, you have to spend a good deal of time deciding what type of person you need for every job description and then going out there and finding the correct match. Or, you could develop them from inside the business. This is the preferred approach, but sometimes you need to kickstart the process by finding someone from outside.

- **Develop accountability:** You, first and foremost, have to get your senior people engaged and onboard as far as the business's goals are concerned before involving the others. The reason for this is that the seniors, be they managers or otherwise, have to set the tone and be an example, just like you do. And, because you may not be employee-facing every day, it's essential that your senior people step into that void you've left seamlessly. The example that juniors see emanating from you should be exactly what they see from the other senior people.

In the final analysis, it's all about developing teams.

Developing Teams

The following are some characteristics of the situation when new teams get together, be it in a job, sporting, or social environment:

- There are high levels of excitement.
- There are high levels of energy and performance.
- Everyone is keen to get on with the job.
- With some, there may be a bit of hesitancy, as they may not feel quite certain what's expected of them.
- Others may slowly start to test the water, so you may have a situation characterized by excitement mingled with tension.

The challenge for the leader is to show what they're doing here and what their purpose, their vision is. To this point, it's important to understand the Tuckman model.

The Tuckman model of team development posits that every team goes through four stages during their development—Forming, Storming, Norming, and Performing. In short, each phase is as follows:

- **Forming:** The team acts as individuals, and there is generally a lack of understanding of each person's roles and responsibilities.
- **Storming:** People start jockeying for position, whether formally or informally, leading to conflict in the process.
- **Norming:** There's great clarity about team roles and individual roles.

- **Performing:** The group has a shared vision and a clear strategy for moving ahead. There is still conflict, but it's handled responsibly (*Forming, Storming, Norming, and Performing. Tuckman's Model for Nurturing a Team to High Performance*, 2020).

You cannot escape going through all four stages. The challenge is to make sure that you get to the Performing stage as quickly as possible. If you get stuck in Storming, it may lead to a lot of damage that may be difficult to fix later. Already, in the Forming stage, everyone needs to understand their role and how it links to the vision. They must be clear on their individual roles and responsibilities. A great way to go about doing this is with the "I SEE/HEAR/FEEL Brainstorm."

How does this work? To get clear on your vision you need to:

- Communicate to the team the vision and the plan to get there even better, discuss the vision and plan and seek their input.
- Be specific and include the problem you're trying to solve and how you'll measure success.

To identify how everyone will contribute you:

- Ask team members to share their strengths and ask them to consider how their role will help to achieve the vision.
- Do this with one-on-one conversations, and then discuss it as a group together.

You then develop the team's norms by:

- Conducting a SEE/HEAR/FEEL brainstorming exercise with the team.
- Ask the team, when you imagine a successful team, what behaviors will you SEE, what words will you HEAR from each other, and how will you and the team FEEL.
- If this is done properly, you should start seeing the beginnings of a cohesive team. However, as I said— every team WILL go through the Storming stage because of the following:
- People are jostling for power and trying to figure out their true role.
- Some may try to stamp their authority onto the team.
- So, some may be fighting for power, while others may be sitting back or withdrawing.
- You may also see some overlap of responsibility.

The reason for this, generally, is because of a lack of clarity in communication. In actual fact, it's because the team has lost sight of their collective vision. The challenge for the leader is to manage the conflict and to shorten this stage as much as possible.

To do this you may consider the following:

- Revisit what you did in the Forming stage.
- Talk (again) about behaviors that are important and that will lead to team success.

- Revisit roles and responsibilities. It's fine if you didn't get this right 100% in the first round.
- Talk about how people communicate, the levels and methods of communication.
- Use the START/STOP/CONTINUE technique. Discuss the team norms and consider what you still need to START. Are there behaviors to STOP? And remember to celebrate what you are doing well with CONTINUE.

As the leader, it's important to spend the maximum amount of time possible with your time during this stage. Another good idea is to use a profiling tool such as DISC or Myers Briggs or Team Roles to understand each other's communication styles. These are freely available on the internet. I generally prefer to have my people do all three.

The Meyers Briggs test is a good indicator of psychological type and preferences. The DISC test is a good indicator of personality types. The team roles test is a good indicator of the role that you would like to play in a team context. Undertaking these tests is an important aid to team building. Once they've been done, the results should be communicated to everyone, as long as people agree.

This will allow people to understand how others like to be communicated with, why they act the way they do, and what their role could be in a team context.

Characteristics of the Norming and Performing stages are:

- People getting on with their work.
- Everything starts to look pretty normal.

- People are more comfortable and know what they have to do on a daily basis.
- They're all contributing to the vision.
- Norming is very similar to Performing, with the main difference being a higher degree of trust in Performing. As mentioned, this doesn't mean that there won't be conflict.

The leader's role during these stages is to keep talking about the vision, because the danger is that anything can trigger a fallback to Storming. So, issues should not be left to fester, but must be brought into the open and discussed. Keep on asking:

- Is our vision still relevant?
- What has changed in our environment?
- What is changing in our team and will it be a barrier to performance?
- What can we do about it? (Blaikie, 2019).

The bottom line when it comes to leading and developing teams is emotional intelligence—in the next chapter we'll discuss this in greater depth. In Chapter 4, we'll also discuss team-building in more detail.

2

EMOTIONAL INTELLIGENCE FOR MODERN LEADERS

"Every problem is a gift—without problems we would not grow."

 –Anthony Robbins

Why Emotional Intelligence?

A successful business leader is a people manager, not just a boss. She's a friend, mentor, and motivator, but won't shy away from enforcing discipline and the correct work ethic. Businesses are indeed set up to make profit, but leaders must understand that teams are made up of humans and managing a team well reflects on the business' level of productivity.

We spoke about teams and developing teams in the previous chapter. Every team is unique in its own way because every team is made up of different people. For this reason, emotional intelligence is important to discern the morale and general outlook of the team while keeping the business afloat. Every successful business has emotional intelligence. Emotional Intelligence (EI) is part of the DNA of any business. And it starts with the leader.

EI versus EQ

Emotional intelligence (EI) is the capability to understand and manage your own and other people's emotions, to discriminate between different emotions, and to name them appropriately. So, people with a high degree of EI know and understand themselves and how they're feeling, and how these feelings and associated emotions can affect other people.

Emotional quotient (EQ), on the other hand, is a testing measurement of our ability to understand and apply our own minds. It reveals how well we learn to manage the negative and positive effects of our emotions so that we know how to apply them going forward (*Keys to Healthier Mind Development*, 2021).

For the purposes of this book, our focus is on EI.

How EI Works

It's generally recognized that having high levels of EI is important for proper leadership as it makes for a more even handed style of leadership. In fact, situational leadership theory, which says that one should adjust one's leadership style to the exigencies of every situation or individual, means that EI plays a central role in leadership.

When Peter Salovey and John D. Mayer coined the term "emotional intelligence" in the 1990s, they didn't know that it would become a household name in the decades to come. Now, it's studied by leaders in business and other aspects of life, including religion and politics.

Emotional Intelligence by Daniel Goleman was first published in 1995. The book, which promoted the concept that EI is more important than IQ in determining success in life, sold five million copies in the first five years of publication. Goleman identified five key elements to EI and posits that the more a leader manage these elements, the higher his or her degree of EI:

- Empathy
- Motivation
- Self-awareness
- Self-regulation
- Social skills

Empathy

Empathy is critical for a leader to manage a successful team. It helps them develop the people on their team. Consider again the team development interventions discussed in Chapter 1. Do you think a leader without empathy would be able to do that well? Good leaders are good listeners and can give constructive and useful feedback.

There are various ways in which one can improve their levels of empathy:

- **Be responsive to feelings:** If you notice an employee being disappointed about an instruction that you gave that may take away some of his or her free time, show sympathy and try to make up for it in some

way. The point is that you should show that you
notice the person's emotions.

- **Put yourself in the other person's shoes:** Try and
understand other people's perspectives on certain
situations. Not everyone will feel the same about
things as you do. There may be good reasons for this.
Try to fathom these.

- **Be sensitive to body language:** Determining how
people feel based on their body language is actually
quite easy. Try to understand why the individual in
front of you is consistently not looking you in the
eye, or keeping her arms crossed. Is there something
in your demeanor that may come across as
threatening or intimidating? There are many courses
available on interpreting body language, and they're
as close as the internet.

- **Listen, really listen:** Empathetic leaders know how
to do active listening, i.e. by repeating or
paraphrasing what an individual has said to them in
some way or another to show that they've
understood the essence of the message. This also
shows respect.

Motivation

Self-motivated leaders work relentlessly toward their goals–
something that we discuss later in this book. They also show
extremely high standards and are proud of the quality of their
own and their people's work.

We also touched on motivation in the previous chapter. It's
important to understand that motivating people isn't a one-off

event–it has to become a way of life in your organization, or else your people may start seeing you as being erratic. Keep those energy levels up! Other ways of improving your motivation include:

- **Learn from setbacks:** Every failure or disappointment has a lesson that can be learned from it, no matter how small. Always look for the positive in a setback. If you make this a way of life, it'll also permeate through to the rest of your team. Speak of facing "challenges," not "problems."
- **Do root cause analysis to find out why you're struggling with something:** Sometimes we forget why it is that we fell in love with our jobs in the first place. Use the "Five Whys" technique to interrogate the cause of the problem. Start by asking why you feel the way you do, and then similarly interrogate every answer till you've followed the causes down five "whys." This is a trick that works almost without fail, and can be usefully applied to many problem-solving and decision-making situations. For more detail on problem-solving, read Chapter 9.
- **Make sure that your goals are challenging:** Despite the hard work that it entails, people are generally not motivated by mundane goals.
- **Know your leadership style:** There are many tools out there that you can take to do an assessment of your leadership style and to understand what your gaps may be.
- **Be positive, even if you don't feel it:** Motivated leaders are generally optimistic, and if you act

positively in front of your people, the positive
feedback that you'll invariably get is likely to also
boost you. It's important to not hide the fact that
you're also human from your people, but on the
other hand, they shouldn't get the impression that
you're constantly down in the dumps while
expecting them to stay motivated. Ain't happening!

Self-awareness

Self-awareness means knowing yourself, your strengths,
and your weaknesses, and being humble. In the 21st century,
4IR environment of leadership, autocratic macho man leadership styles no longer impress people. There may be a role for
that still in the military, but in general, people are much more
motivated by the Elon Musks and Steve Jobs of the world today.

Things that you can do to improve self-awareness include:

- **Examine yourself:** When you're upset, try to analyze
  what the real reasons are, not just the symptoms. Is
  it rational? Is it mature? Would your role-model act
  in a similar way? Practicing yoga or tai chi is a great
  way of tapping into your inner core and becoming
  more self-aware.
- **Keep a journal:** Spending some time every day to
  keep a journal is a great way of enhancing your self-
  awareness. Writing down your feelings and
  experiences of the day forces you to re-examine
  them, as well as your specific reactions.

Self-regulation

Self-regulation is exactly what the term says–regulating your own behavior. Thinking before you act. Not acting when your emotions are too aroused. Leaders who don't regulate themselves effectively tend to make hasty or emotional decisions, often not based on their or the organization's values. The buzzword here is control.

Ways to improve self-regulation include:

- **Practice calmness:** Take a few deep breaths before responding to a statement or question. Become attuned to the emotions that you're experiencing. It's also better, if you can, to respond on paper rather than verbally, as that often tends to make you reconsider the veracity of your response. Always ask yourself, "Will this response be fair?"
- **Stick to your values:** Remember the values that we spoke of in the last chapter? The ones that you developed with your team? Are you certain about the areas in which you definitely will not compromise? Make sure you make the right choice and that it's aligned with the values of your organization. Nothing demoralizes people faster than if their leader expects them to act in a certain way but has a different set of rules for themselves.
- **Keep yourself accountable:** A leader is always accountable. You can delegate responsibility but never accountability. The buck stops with you. Admit your mistakes if you're wrong and accept

accountability for your team's mistakes. Face the consequences, whatever they are.

Social Skills

Good leaders are invariably good communicators. I don't mean that they have to compete with a Bill Clinton or a Ronald Reagan as to having the gift of the gab, but they're not scared to talk in public and they have the ability to translate their thoughts effectively.

Such leaders are good change managers and get stuck in the details of the work with their people because they speak the same language.

Ways to develop social skills include:

- **Praise others:** One of the easiest ways to motivate people but at the same time to lay the foundation for good communication is to praise people. There's an old saying that goes, "Try to catch people doing something right." This is much more difficult than catching them doing something wrong, but in the end, it's a much more fulfilling exercise.
- **Manage conflicts:** Conflict management is an essential communication skill for managers. There are many courses that teach you how to do this.
- **Improve your skills:** If you feel you have to improve your communications skills, there are many courses available. Or you can join organizations like Toastmasters (*Emotional Intelligence in Leadership*, n.d.).

So, EI skills can be learned. Studies have shown that there are two areas of learning these skills (Brown, 2021):

- **Cognitive learning:** Intellectually understanding these concepts that we discussed above and knowing that you need to develop them but not making the leap to be able to do it.
- **Emotional learning:** Unlearning old habits and relearning new ones. The basis of learning EI is through creating new habits and by enhancing your self-discipline.
- EI skills are vital for properly managing conflict within your business.

Solving Conflicts in Your Team

There are many reasons for conflict within teams:

- **Differences in background and education:** These differences may relate to gender, ethnicity, religion, political views, or lower or higher levels of education. Whatever the context, it results in people having different perspectives on virtually everything. This has a major impact on how we relate to and interact with others.
- **Differences in approach:** Factors like arrogance, cynicism, irritability, a demanding demeanor, and other things can all contribute to an attitude of negativity. This, in turn, impacts effective communication, as very few people like to be around and communicate with negative people. People who

constantly complain and look for problems in others or the work situation make cooperation very difficult.

- **Differences in work style:** Because we're all different, we all have different approaches to our work. Some work fast, others slowly. Some are very methodical and like to plan things out first. Others like to just jump in and start. Some like to get the job done in teams. Others may prefer to work on tasks by themselves. This is related to the way people learn, as well. According to the Kolb model, people learn in three ways and although we all go through all three ways of learning, we each have a preferred way. We're either visual learners, meaning that we like to be shown how things are done, auditory learners, meaning that we like to listen to explanations about how things work, or kinesthetic learners, meaning that we like to jump in and start experimenting.
- **Differences in ways of cooperation:** Some people are very cooperative in the work environment while others are extremely competitive. To those with a more cooperative slant, people who are competitive and who may be aggressively pursuing their own agenda at the expense of working together in a civilized manner may be very draining. If taken to an extreme, it can create paralysis in the work environment, because one group is aggressive and can't get help from the other group, who may just isolate themselves at the expense of the organization achieving its goals.

Consequences of Personality Conflicts

Continued personality conflicts within the workspace can lead to serious consequences, including:

- **Stress:** It's common knowledge that continued long-term high-stress levels can have serious negative impacts on an individual's physical and mental health. Not only does constant tension and anxiety in the team lead to stress, but often people leave their jobs when the situation becomes too unbearable.
- **Productivity:** The essence of teamwork and collaboration is all about better productivity. This is, after all, why we put people together in teams, so that the impact of the whole can be bigger and better than the individual parts. But, when there are individual clashes, the outputs and outcomes of whatever project it is that the team is focused on are likely to suffer. In the process, the productivity and morale of the whole team are likely to be negatively impacted.

Handling Conflict

As we illustrated with the stages that teams go through in their development, especially as far as the Storming stage is concerned, workplace conflict is unavoidable. Your job as the leader is to minimize it and to ensure that it's handled correctly. Things to keep in mind in that respect include:

- As the leader, when things don't go the way they should, you should always question your own leadership style first. Is there something that you did, some example that you set that may have contributed to the situation? Remember that your way is not necessarily the only way, or even the correct way. This is a sign of having a high level of EI.
- As we said earlier, people have different perspectives. You have to accept that and understand it. Handling different perspectives differently is the essence of situational leadership.
- Apart from different perspectives, people also have different personalities. These differences in personalities, if handled correctly, can strengthen the cohesion and output of a team.
- But, when personality conflicts reach the point where it impacts the people, output, and productivity of your organization negatively, you have to stand up and address it.

Personality conflict is generally a manager or leader's worst nightmare in the workplace. The reason for this is, of course, that it is not always easy to fathom what the reasons are behind a personality clash. Conflicts can often be handled by creating a situation where all the relevant individuals practice under-standing, acceptance, and professionalism. But, because emotions are involved, this isn't always that easy. Ways to foster understanding and acceptance include the following:

- **Remain professional:** One of the best ways to

address conflict is to watch the tone of your communication. We'll get to communication in more detail in the next section, but it's important for everyone to remain calm and courteous to ensure that confrontation is avoided. Everyone needs to understand that conflict will occur in the workplace and that we don't all have to like each other. Remaining professional and civil in communication can go a long way toward resolving conflicts or nipping them in the bud before they even occur.

- **Get to the root cause:** Despite the difficulty, it's important to get to the bottom of conflicts. Otherwise, you may just be addressing the symptoms of the problem, which will inevitably result in the same issue arising again. Practice the 5 Whys that we mentioned earlier. Have a proper conversation with each person involved. Get a neutral outsider, if necessary, to mediate the situation, if your people think that you may not be objective enough about the specific issue at stake.

- **Acceptance:** Sometimes, just accepting that we all have our differences may go a long way to resolving conflicts. To this end, it may be well worth your while to invest some time in doing the personality profiles with your team that I covered in Chapter 1, so that everyone can understand each other and why they act the ways that they do better.

- **Escalation:** If you're the top dog in the organization, then things have already escalated to your level. If not, it is possible to escalate it further up the chain of management for resolution. This is generally not

the wisest thing to do unless it's a situation that is
really out of control. The reason why I advise against
this is because of trust. If you can't resolve the
situation and it becomes evident that you have to
escalate it, it may impact the trust relationship with
your team. Other options, of course, also include
inter-team or inter-departmental transfers of
troublesome individuals and, in worst-case
scenarios, getting rid of someone completely.
However, in most jurisdictions and industries, there
are strict labor law directives that have to be
followed to "rehabilitate" someone before going to
the drastic step of dismissing them (Scuderi, n.d.).

Effective Communication

Effective communication is the golden thread that runs through
every successful enterprise. We've already shown how ineffective communication can result in conflict, and how being an
effective communicator can help to address conflict.

Apart from solving conflicts, communication is an important tool to ensure people stay motivated and that business
goals get achieved. The most successful companies are those
where their communication structures, formally and informally, work well. Leaders who show by example that they value
effective communication help to engender trust in themselves
and the organization, show that they value two-way communication, and in the process, that they value the inputs of their
subordinates and peers. There are several ways to go about this:

- **Active listening:** What is active listening? It is

showing to the other party that you're listening intently to the message that they're trying to convey to you by engaging in the process—not by talking, but through your emotions and body language. Ways to do that include making and keeping eye contact, responding appropriately by nodding or making some small verbal interjections, not interrupting the speaker, and by, at regular intervals, paraphrasing to show that you have been listening with phrases like, "So, if I understand you correctly you are saying..."

- **The correct method for the audience and the occasion:** In all organizations, communication is done through physical interaction, telephone, e-mails, internet (Zoom, etc.), and maybe some social media like Slack or Whatsapp. It's important to know what method works best for what occasion, and that verbal communication also involves body language. Face-to-face communication is always best when it can be done, but is not always practical. Understand the power of visually representing data through the use of charts, maps, images, and graphs. Getting a team collaboration app, of which there are many, can also be a powerful tool to help your team members collaborate on different activities and projects.

- **Be clear and concise:** People appreciate brevity, be it in verbal or non-verbal communication. Make a point of getting your message across clearly and remind yourself that everyone's time is precious.

- **Give your undivided attention:** Don't let yourself be

sidetracked by things or other people when someone is talking to you. Constantly looking at your phone is a big no-no. Maintain eye contact and show the person that you respect them enough to listen with your undivided attention.

- **Plan your message:** Passing along the message is half the issue. You also have to think about what you want the team to do with the information once they've received it. After all, you're not communicating just for the sake of it, are you? What must people remember? What must they do? There must be some sort of actionable part to the message.

- **Be confident and persuasive:** To communicate effectively, i.e. communicating the correct message, also means showing patience, confidence, and persuasiveness. Ways to do that are to be friendly, smile, keep your arms uncrossed, maintain an erect posture, keep eye contact, and ensure that devices don't get in the way.

- **Manage time properly:** Coffee breaks are a nice way to ensure that people get the rest that they need during the day, but that the time is also being used productively. Well-managed coffee breaks can be mini team-building exercises where people are encouraged to talk about specific things. So, working, productivity and coffee breaks aren't necessarily mutually exclusive, and can dovetail nicely with each other to contribute to team bonding.

- **Do team-building:** Well-structured team-building exercises are a good way to develop *esprit de corps* and to encourage motivation within the team. While the leader should take part in facilitating some of the exercises, it's also important that outside assistance is solicited to generate some new ideas. Sometimes team-building may also be coupled with strategic planning exercises to kill the proverbial two birds with one stone.

- **Show appreciation:** People always perform better when they're appreciated. This can be done formally, by having something like employee of the month awards, which is done publicly. But showing appreciation should also become a daily, if not hourly, way of encouraging and motivating people. Just that small "thank you" or "well done" goes a long way. It's easy to catch people doing something wrong. As I said previously, it's much more difficult, but more rewarding, to catch them doing something right. For that, you have to actually look for reasons to praise them.

- **Encourage two-way communication:** Productivity and morale are boosted when employees feel that they're encouraged to have their say. Not only that, but that management listens to their input and implements their suggestions. As a leader, you have to have some sort of task management system which records all input to help increase overall communication and productivity.

- **Have one-on-one discussions:** Group discussions are good, but there also have to be one-on-one discussions between the team leader and the employees in the business. They're a great source of motivation and also help employees know how they're performing and where course-corrections may be made. These discussions should be held at least quarterly. One of the biggest mistakes that companies make is to only have a one-on-one discussion with an employee during the annual performance assessment. This may be the first opportunity for the employee to get wind of the fact that management isn't impressed with his or her performance. More regular interventions allow for smaller course corrections as required, resulting in less of a shock to the individual once a year! It's also important to listen carefully to what the employee says during these discussions.

We've touched on most of these in the preceding sections, but in summary - to develop effective communication skills means working on the following:

- **Be aware of your body language and its impact:** Although this is very much related also to cultural factors, ensure that you understand how it can come across when you fold your arms (defensive posture), keep your hands behind your body (confidence), fiddle with your watch or ring (nervousness), clench your fists (anger), or squeeze your hands (soothing). These are the so-called universal body language signs that most people tend to understand.
- **Listen actively:** Completely focus on the individual speaking with you and give them your undivided attention.

- **Deliver your message with confidence:** Deliver a strong, actionable message by being patient, methodical, and assured.
- **Keep it positive:** People tend to rally around positivity and reject negativity. In a team context, a positive frame of mind is important for employee motivation and productivity. It is the leader who sets the tone in this regard (Hasyap, n.d.).

Effective communication is also an essential skill if you want to be able to delegate properly.

The Art of Delegation

If you run a business, there's no way you can get everything done by yourself. Of necessity, you have to be able to delegate. There's no one-size-fits-all approach to delegation, but it is important to keep a number of points in mind.

Firstly, delegation can be an extremely fulfilling experience, as it allows you to develop and grow your employees. After all, how are they ever going to learn the ropes if you don't give them work to do? And "giving them work to do" amounts to delegation.

Second, remember that you can delegate responsibility but never accountability. As the leader, you always remain accountable for the outcomes of your team and your business. As a simple example—you can delegate the responsibility for running the company's finances to your financial manager, but you remain accountable for the financial success of your business. In turn, the financial manager can delegate the responsibility for maintaining the general ledger to a finance clerk, but she remains accountable for the successful running of the whole finance department.

Third, you have to think before delegating something. There has to be a mix between the individual's capabilities, area of work, and the task that is about to be delegated. The individual also needs to have the skills and training to be able to do the work. It's patently unfair to delegate something to an employee who has not the remotest idea of how to go about it. That becomes abdication.

Other things to keep in mind are:

- **Have the right people:** Talent management is one of a leader's most important jobs. You must have the right people in place to delegate to. Those people must be trained. If they cannot be trained, they must be replaced. You have to be able to trust people to be able to do the work that gets delegated to them, or else why did you appoint them in the first place? Delegation becomes easy when you know that your people are trained and trustworthy so that you can delegate with peace of mind.

- **Delegate the correct responsibilities:** It's a true managerial skill to, over time, learn which tasks to delegate and which to not. A good leader knows which tasks to keep to themselves. Again, there's no hard and fast rule, but generally, tasks that are directly related to your accountability should not be delegated. Sub-elements can, of course. As an example—as the CEO of the company the financial success of the enterprise has been given to you as one of your Key Performance Areas (KPAs) by the

Board. It has, in other words, been delegated to you. You cannot delegate the financial success of the organization to your financial manager. However, you can delegate sub-elements of it to her—financial statements drafting, expenditure reporting, financial accounting, etc.

- **Mentor and guide:** I have alluded to this, but you should take care not to abdicate when you delegate. There should always be clear and concise instructions about how things should be done, or rather, not how it should be done exactly, but about the outcomes that you desire. You have to set your expectations clearly to ensure that there's no performance/expectations mismatch. These guidelines should include statements about the overall goal of the task, the required outcome, the importance of it, a target date for completion, and some sort of quality standard guideline as to the quality of the output.

- **Focus on the outcome required (rather than on how to go about it):** This can be a bit tricky and will depend on the maturity of the individual to whom the task is delegated, as well as his or her level of expertise and experience. It's good to only specify the outcomes expected when delegating to an experienced employee. When the person is still new to the job, you should accompany that with much more detail. In the process, you should take care not to micromanage. Most experienced individuals hate it when their manager keeps looking over their shoulder the whole time to see if the job is being done. On the other hand, ongoing support and clear communication during the process are important, and the employee must understand that they can always come back for more instruction or to get things cleared up. Youngsters may need to be managed more tightly.

- **Delegate what is in the interests of the team/business:** Delegation is part of the art of making your team more experienced and successful in the process contributing to business success. On the main, people enjoy being given challenging goals to pursue to prove their worth. If you don't have such people, you have to revisit your approach to talent management, or perhaps, look at yourself and your managerial and leadership abilities.

The art of delegation is all about improving the efficiency and effectiveness of an enterprise. It's not about seeing how much of your work you can give to others to do. There is a science behind it, but in the main, it's an art that comes with experience. It comes down to:

- Getting rid of as many routine tasks that you can so that you can focus on strategic thinking and the big picture.
- Understanding that you remain accountable for the work delegated.
- Increasing the responsibility of employees so that it can contribute to their own development, morale, and job satisfaction.
- Understanding that certain tasks lend themselves to

delegation and others do not. Delegate work that can be more efficiently done by someone else.

- Delegating a mixture of tasks so that employees can see that you don't just get rid of things that you don't like doing.
- Specifying tasks properly and ensuring that people have the skills and tools to do the job as and when they receive it (*The Art of Effective Delegation*, n.d.).

In the next chapter, we move on to what many consider to be the essence of small business success, i.e. the financial planning and everything related to it.

FINANCIAL PLANNING FOR SMALL BUSINESSES

"Business opportunities are like buses, there's always another one coming."
  –Richard Branson

Plans aren't made in the air. They have to be embodied in the strategic goals and objectives of the business. Financial planning means putting on paper the activities, resources, equipment, and materials needed by the business. It first starts with strategy, though.

The Strategy

This chapter is about financial planning, but one of the biggest mistakes that companies, big or small, make is to dive straight into financial planning without hinging it on a strategy. Most organizations "follow the book" on strategy management and utilize many resources to communicate the strategy, translate the strategy into objectives, cascade the objectives down the hierarchy, develop action plans to achieve the objectives, measure progress through key performance indicators (KPIs) or some other measures, and reward performance, etc.

What many business leaders don't understand, however, is that strategy and strategic planning is not pure science. It's both a science and an art. The science part is well-established and there are many books available on strategic planning method-ologies and techniques. What people tend to forget, though, is that strategy is about changing organizations. And people have a natural tendency to want to resist change. So the "art" part has to do with managing change, about changing people's perceptions and behaviors. One could even say that this is the most important part of strategy and strategy implementation. And this is most probably the reason why strategies often don't get fully implemented, or implemented at all, in organizations.

There are many definitions of strategy–I look at only a few.

According to J. Loewen (1997), "Strategy is a process to lead change. You need a view of the future and then an under-standing of the sort of skills or competencies necessary to operate in that future."

According to Pfeifer et al (1985), "Strategic planning is the process by which the guiding members of an organization envi-sion its future and develop the necessary procedures and opera-tions to achieve that future."

Johnson and Scoles (2008) define strategy as, "The direction and scope of an organization over the long-term: which achieves advantage for the organization through its configura-tion of resources within a challenging environment, to meet the needs of markets and to fulfill stakeholder expectations."

In other words, strategy is all about answering:

- What direction do we want to pursue over the long term?
- What are the markets that we want to pursue it in?
- Within those markets, how can we perform better than the competition?
- What resources will we need to be successful in competing in those markets?
- What matters in our business context will impact how we perform in those markets, both opportunities and threats?
- What are the expectations and values of our stakeholders for our performance in these markets?

If these are important questions to be answered in the strategy formulation process, then one could say that developing a strategy for a business must be done with the following objectives in mind:

- To make sure that your business's future is under control.
- To enhance communication in the business.
- To focus and grow yourself and your people toward the common goal.
- To set yourself apart from the competition.

The aim, therefore, is to be better than your competitors and to have an advantage in creating customer value. To do this the Balanced Scorecard is a very useful construct.

The Balanced Scorecard (BSC) was developed in the early nineties by Kaplan and Norton to do exactly what I described in the preceding paragraphs–to develop and implement strategy and to identify the relevant objectives needed for success.

Kaplan and Norton realized early on that one had to look at other strategic measures apart from just the traditional financial measures of success, like Return on Equity (ROE), Return on Investment (ROI), and others. Instead, one must take a more balanced view, because although the financial measures may be the ones that eventually count to determine whether you are winning or failing as a business, there are many other measures that are "rolled up" into creating successful financial outcomes.

The value of the BSC, therefore, is that it provides a way in which to connect the organization's vision, mission, strategy, projects, and objectives across the company so that people can all see in a transparent manner how what they're doing is contributing to organizational success.

BSC recommends looking at an organization according to four different perspectives to help develop objectives, measures (KPIs), targets, and initiatives (programs) relative to those views.

- **Financial:** This is the top perspective into which the other three perspectives roll up, and considers an organization's financial performance and the use of its financial capabilities.
- **Customer:** This perspective takes a view of how the customer sees the organization and which objectives and initiatives should be undertaken to make the customer happy. It includes marketing.
- **Internal business process:** This addresses the company's business processes in an integrated view, from raw materials delivered to sales; everything

related to the product or service that the
organization produces.

- **Learning and growth:** This perspective considers
infrastructure, human capital, technology, and other
capabilities that are required to make the
organization perform. It's especially related to
people's development in the company (*Balanced
Scorecard Basics*, n.d.).

The final output of a strategic planning exercise using the
BSC approach will therefore be the following:

- A strategy map that shows the four perspectives.
- Within each perspective, the goals and objectives to
be pursued, with associated KPIs and targets.
- The initiatives that support the work within each
perspective.

A note on terminology at this point–I sometimes use goals
and objectives interchangeably, but that's not quite correct. In
the hierarchy of "things" to be produced by a company, the
highest order is Outcomes. Outcomes are broken down into
Outputs (goals), and Outputs, in turn, may be broken down into
Objectives. Objectives are again broken down into tasks and so
on. We'll cover this in a bit more detail in the next section.

Goals and objectives should have KPIs and targets. An
example of a KPI is "the number of widgets produced daily."
The target may be 200. This will typically be a goal under the
business process perspective of the BSC. Objectives under this
goal may be "number of blue widgets made," and "number of

black widgets made." The overall Outcome of this process may be "successful widget production."

Initiatives, also sometimes called programs in organizations, are the longer-term projects that support the work done within each perspective. In the example above, we may have to invest in new equipment to meet our KPI target of 200 widgets per day. This, then, is an initiative that will be assigned to an individual that runs throughout that whole perspective in order to ensure that the outputs (goals) and outcomes are attained.

Let's consider goals and objectives in more detail.

What are Business Goals and Objectives?

Goals tend to be qualitative, while objectives are normally quantitative, although exceptions are possible. There is close alignment between your goals and the outcomes to be achieved, which in turn should all be aligned with the organization's vision.

An example of a business goal could be, "to expand from $100,000 turnover to $1,000,000 turnover in the next five years." Business goals say what the destination is and the timeline to get there. It has to do with effectiveness, i.e. doing the right things.

Objectives, on the other hand, are more focused on efficiencies, i.e. doing things correctly. This is aligned to the daily metrics that revolve around numbers of customers, numbers of products, revenue, etc. Objectives, therefore, are specific procedures for achieving a goal. They're the steps that you need to take in order to achieve your desired goals. For instance, if your goal is to expand your business from $100,000 to $1,000,000 turnover in the next five years, you could have the following objectives:

- To market the business more aggressively to attract 15% more customers.
- To spend 2% of turnover on a customer loyalty program.
- To develop online marketing capabilities that will result in 10% more SEO hits in six months' time.
- To research and analyze possible growth opportunities such as acquisitions, mergers, etc.
- To introduce new products and services at a rate of two every six months.
- To open more offices in various locations before year-end.

Your objectives say what steps to take and when. So, goals and objectives work in harmony to ensure that you achieve business success.

- Goals say where you want to get to and objectives give you the how.
- Goals contribute to effectiveness, objectives to efficiency.
- Objectives are more detailed than goals and generally include dates and performance metrics.

Next, you have to compile your goals and objectives into your business plan. It's generally a good idea not to have too many business goals if you're a small business. A rule of thumb is anywhere between four and eight. If you have less, you have to wonder whether you're trying to achieve anything. More than that, and you may be overburdening your people because, remember, every goal gets broken down into objectives, and there may be a number of them per goal. Some guidelines for determining your goals include the following (many of the answers to these questions will already be forthcoming from your strategy BSC exercise):

- Set numbers for your annual revenue in the short, medium, and long terms.
- Consider what market share you want in each of those time frames.
- Consider the number of employees that you want to have for each of those time frames.
- Evaluate whether you'll concentrate on one market niche or whether you'll expand.
- Also, consider whether such expansion will include geographical expansion.
- Consider your organizational structure and lines of responsibility.
- Consider your funding model.
- Consider your business model. Will you remain a private company, NGO, NPO, or go public eventually?
- Finally, before including your goals and related objectives into your business plan you have to make sure that they are SMART (Martins, n.d.). SMART stands for Specific, Measurable, Action-oriented, Relevant, and Timebound.

So much, then, for strategy and the related goals. I hope you can see by now why it's important to first undergo a rigorous strategic planning exercise in your company before diving straight into financial planning. Moving onto that subject, let's consider why financial planning is important.

Importance of Financial Planning

You now know what you want to achieve, financially and otherwise. You now have to decompose all of that into financial targets, policies, techniques, projects, and budgets for the short and medium-term. Financial planning should also be done for the longer term, but budgeting is normally only undertaken for the short and medium terms. This is important to do because:

- It ensures that there will be sufficient funds available to pursue your goals.
- It ensures that there is harmony between managing your inputs and outputs.
- It ensures that there's transparency to providers of funds about how the funds are to be managed.
- It supports development programs of both the organization and its people to support long-term sustainability.
- Having sufficient funds available may serve as a hedge against changing business conditions brought about by changes in the context, i.e, the external environment within which the organization operates.
- It ensures that weaknesses may be addressed and opportunities may be pursued.

If these, then, are the reasons why it's important to do financial planning, one may say that related objectives of financial planning are the following:

- **Ensuring that funds are available:** This includes forecasts as to requirements of funds for different purposes, be it for projects, long-term asset replacement, working (operating) capital requirements, etc. Proper planning ensures that funds are timely made available as per the plan, and as per the exigencies imposed by the strategy.
- **Ensuring that the funds are available at the right time:** Insufficient cash flow when it's required has been a major death blow to countless organizations. It's crucial that the right funds are delivered at the right time.
- **Developing the capital structure:** How funds are comprised in an organization is vital. Is it composed of partner funding, bank funding, shareholder funding, or other options? Most organizations use a hybrid approach, but that requires proper planning because every contributor of funds wants their slice of the pie and wants to rest assured that their contribution will be optimally utilized. This includes matters like debt-equity ratio for both the short-term and long-term.
- **Avoiding unnecessary surplus funds:** Whereas a shortage of funds may be terminal, a surplus of funds at the wrong time is also not a good idea, as that means that the organization is not optimally employing its resources to generate more money,

either by proper investment or capital structuring. In short, it's a waste of money.

The process of getting this sorted is the following, in very abridged format:

- Prepare the sales forecast/conjecture.
- Decide how this translates into funds required–fixed assets and working capital.
- Determine how much of what is required can be financed internally.
- The gap that typically arises from the previous step then leads us to consider various external financing options. Part of this will be to consider the cost of capital from the various potential sources.
- Reconcile the various options and then develop spending plans based on the above (*Financial Planning*, 2020).

Let's now move from the generic to the specific. You have your strategy developed. You've set goals and objectives and you have a fairly good idea of where you want to go financially, considering the guidelines in this section. You now need to create and implement your action plan.

Create the Financial Action Plan

There are several principles to consider here as you go forward:

- **Involve your people from the start:** Ideally, many of your people should already be involved in your strategic planning process. This may not always be practical, depending on the size of your organization, but involving your people as early as possible ensures that they buy into the plan. It also ensures that all ideas are considered and that everyone understands what is expected of them.

- **Be specific about the details:** We discussed this at some length under the goals section. Typically, you'll have a one-page spreadsheet that lists actions, linked to a KPI (or more than one), names of those responsible, and the timeline for execution indicated. More details on each activity can be included as appendices/footnotes.
- **Include a time horizon:** The action plans can cover one or multiple years. As you go further into the future, details will become more vague, especially as far as the budget is concerned.
- **Allocate resources:** The reason why many plans fail is that people aren't given the resources to implement them. And time is also a resource. A useful tool to apply in this regard is the RASCI matrix. This shows who will be:
- Responsible—who does the job.
- Accountable—who manages the job.
- Support—who provides support.
- Consulted—who may be consulted. These would be individuals with expert domain knowledge on the subject, internal to or external to the company.
- Informed—who must be informed and kept abreast of the development of this initiative.
- **Develop the tracking program:** You need to have a

sort of mechanism to track progress on your plan. This could include milestones of when you will reach certain measures that can be quantified, like revenue or margin. There should also be some system as to how feedback should be given, through meetings or otherwise. People must know that there's a mechanism that they can fall back on to get course correction or guidance if they're struggling.

- **Communication:** The plan needs to be communicated down to the lower levels. Everyone must understand how it works and what their specific contributions are to the plan (*7 Steps to Create an Action Plan for Your Business Strategy*, n.d.).

Know the Financial Situation of the Business

In order to give an idea of the things to consider when investigating the financials of a company, I use the example of considering buying an existing business, as opposed to starting afresh. Many of the terminology and approaches are the same, but generally speaking, if you buy an existing business, you're likely to run a steep learning curve as to all the financial information that you need to consider. This is because, in most cases, not all, starting your own business is an incremental undertaking that doesn't immediately involve you having to be on top of so many financial variables.

One of the first things to do, of course, is to consider whether the asking price is fair. To do this you should consider issues like the business's financial health, its earnings history, growth potential, and of course, the value of intangible assets, like brand name and market position (also sometimes referred to as intellectual capital).

To get an idea of the financial health of a company, you should obtain its projections of anticipated returns and future financial needs, look at the financial statements like balance sheets, income statements, cash flow statements, footnotes, and tax returns. This will give you a good basis from which to do some financial analysis and to look at the financial ratios to determine business health.

Issues to consider include the following:

- **Inventory levels:** This will depend on whether it's a product or service business. Excessive inventory may include obsolete inventory, and inventory costs money to store. There's also an opportunity cost associated with inventory that doesn't get used. It can also mean that orders aren't being fulfilled as they should, which in turn could mean that there are many dissatisfied customers, which could impact your customer perspective on your BSC.
- **Accounts receivable:** A big debtor's book could mean that customers aren't paying you and that could be underpinned by other factors again. You need to investigate the credit policies, cash collection schedules, accounts receivable ratio, and receivables aging ratio.
- **Net income:** There are some ratios that you need to consider here. The ratio of net income to total assets may indicate whether the company is receiving a favorable rate of return on assets. The gross profit ratio (gross profit to net sales) can be used to do

comparisons of the profit margin with similar companies. The net income ratio (net income to net worth) can show whether you can expect a reasonable profit.

- **Sales activity:** Again, a number of things to consider. If sales are up, look at whether it's because volume is up or whether prices have increased. Also, consider the maturity of the marketplace. If sales are stagnant, it could mean the market has reached a saturation point for that specific product, hence why it is being sold, even if the sales look good.

- **Fixed assets:** Fixed asset levels need to be aligned with the levels of production. If there are more assets than required, it could mean a decline in market demand or an over-investment in assets. Either way, this means that you have money tied up in equipment that you could use better elsewhere.

- **Working capital:** Working capital is calculated by subtracting current liabilities from current assets. An important ratio to also consider is net sales to net working capital. This will show how efficiently working capital is contributing to business objectives. Working capital = cash flow and is vital for business success.

- **Operating environment:** The context of the business is important. Things to consider include whether the business supplies locally or overseas, whether it gets material locally or overseas, whether the product or service will be in demand in five years time, the level of integration, i.e. is the business part of a long sales funnel (perhaps by being a supplier of parts), or is it completely integrated, meaning it makes its own raw materials and uses them to produce the product. Most businesses lie somewhere on a continuum here. The point is that it's important to consider this, because it may have an important bearing on long-term viability. An example—your business may be producing seals for a company that maintains oil pipelines in the Middle East, but in that specific country, the production of LNG is assuming greater importance than oil. What does that mean for the outputs of this company over the long term? (*8 Factors That Determine the Financial Health of a Business*, 2015).

Normally, when you buy a new business, most of the calculations in terms of markup and others are already embedded in the company, although you may want to revisit them once you take over. For both new or old businesses, these ratios are important considerations:

- Mark-up % calculation.
- Gross profit % calculation.
- Break-even turnover calculation.
- Break-even number of units calculation.
- The maximum customer discount % calculation.
- True total cost per unit calculation.

Investments and Savings

You're running your company. Everything is going well. Money is coming in and you may even be a bit cash-flush! What to do with it? Consider these options for using retained income:

- **Improve the business:** Firstly, your strategy should determine what you're going to do with surplus funds. But, if you've already outlined these plans in your BSC, then it could be a worthwhile addition to your company profile to improve the infrastructure, processes, layout, customer appeal, etc. A lot of this will be determined by the type of business you're in, i.e. product or service-oriented. Either way, investing in better customer service is always a winner.
- **Marketing:** We'll cover marketing in more detail later but this is often the nemesis of small businesses, especially new ones. It goes about the old trade-off between investing in marketing and spending that money to improve your product. If you don't have much experience in this, and you have the funds available, it may be worthwhile to consider outsourcing to an agency. It may also be worthwhile to consider improving your SEO capabilities, but that again will depend on the type of market that you are serving. If you're producing a single product for a single client (risky) it may not be worth your effort. If, however, you want to produce and sell the same product to many new customers, then it may be worth your while.
- **Invest in your people:** High employee turnover is

expensive. Training and developing your people will remain one of your most important investments, especially if you're running a small business where everyone has to be on top of their game. In large organizations, there's often some support that can cover for the lack of performance of some employees, but in a small business, there's nowhere to hide! Everyone is customer-facing and everyone has to have customer-handling skills, as just one example.

- **Invest in yourself:** You must make sure that you stay abreast of the latest developments in leadership and management, as well as the things that impact your industry. This can include both formal and informal development, like attending seminars. To further develop yourself, you could consider getting a mentor or business coach. This is especially important if you're unsure about things like strategy, managing conflict with employees, talking to investors, etc.

- **Outsource tasks if you can:** Tasks can be outsourced, but be careful what you consider here. Your core business process can never be outsourced. Peripheral tasks that may be a pain at times may be considered for outsourcing. One example is your HR function. There are many small companies that specialize in providing dedicated support for HR requirements to businesses, from recruitment through to payroll.

- **Retain some cash:** While reinvesting in your business is important, make sure that you have sufficient cash to handle problems that may arise. Insurance policies may cover disasters but some other emergencies may require liquidity for you to cover.

- **Diversify. Or not:** It is all good and well to have an ambition to diversify, but you first need to bed your business down properly. Take care of the essentials first, like your employees and customers, and ensure that your plans to diversify and grow are included in your strategy. That way, once you get to where you should be according to the strategy, and you're happy with present performance, then you can take the next step (Boitnott, 2017).

Running a successful small business means that you have to be successful with the bottom-line. No business can survive indefinitely being in the red all the time. But you can only achieve this by building and maintaining a strong team. Let's see how we can further develop those capabilities in the next chapter.

4

WHAT IS TEAM BUILDING?

"Success is not final; failure is not fatal: it is the courage to
continue that counts."
 –Winston Churchill

In Chapter 1, we touched on the importance of team
development and the different stages a team goes
through in their developmental cycle. In this chapter,
we'll go into this in more detail.

Successful business leaders know how to harness the
uniqueness of an individual to achieve the goals of his business.
Individuals make a team, but a leader builds a team and makes
it productive. Team building is important because it turns a
group of individual contributing employees into a cohesive
team that can make landmark achievements for the business.
In addition, building a team forges stronger, lasting relationships and connections among the members of a group.

Definition of Team Building

Team building is a management technique that's used to align the people with the organization's goals. In the process, and done correctly, it improves the performance and efficiency of the individuals and the group. The aim is alignment with the organization's vision and business objectives.

The whole idea centers around the term "alignment." Aligning people's work, attitude, engagement, output, personal interactions, and communication to the requirements needed to achieve the vision. In the process, several "peripheral" spin-offs are achieved: happier people, better organizational culture, team spirit, a positive work environment, and engaged employees.

Advantages of Team Building

Effective and efficient team building can contribute to the following:

- **Alignment:** We covered this in the last section, but team building is a great contributor to *hoshin kanri*, the Japanese concept of alignment of business strategy so that the individual, the organization's goals, objectives, mission, and vision are clearly defined and aligned with each other.
- **Better change management:** People who are happy and function well in teams adapt better to fluid and changing working conditions. And changing working conditions are the nature of the beast in

2021 and beyond. It's easier for a leader to manage change with engaged employees who understand the business imperatives and each other well.

- **Better problem-solving:** We'll cover problem-solving in more detail in Chapter 9, but people who function well together as a team are more inclined to contribute to solving problems and sharing their views in brainstorming sessions and in other ways of approaching problems. Interestingly enough, in my experience, I've found that doing problem-solving is, by itself, a very useful team building exercise because of the free exchange of thoughts and ideas that happens during the process.

- **Clear roles and responsibilities:** In Chapter 1, we explained the importance of developing clear roles and responsibilities to ensure that role ambiguity is addressed and to remove uncertainty from people about what they're supposed to do. Team building exercises can contribute to this because, by bonding as a team, individuals feel freer to address issues that may be of concern regarding their roles. It's just natural that, as your employees start getting to know each other better, they'll also feel more free to start interrogating their specific roles and may point out where they see role ambiguities or where there may be overlaps in roles and responsibilities. This is something the leader should actively encourage, because it shows that your people are starting to know the organization well.

- **Communication and collaboration:** Because

people get to know each other well, it automatically opens up channels of communication and people feel more inclined to engage with each other.

- **Delegation:** A well-developed team understands how and why tasks get delegated. More importantly, if the team is a cohesive unit, the manager finds it much easier to delegate assignments to the team, knowing that the team has the knowledge and maturity to sub-divide such responsibilities among themselves.

- **Identification of strengths and weaknesses:** Team building can reveal the strengths and weaknesses of individuals. In Chapter 1, we explained how certain instruments could be used to understand individuals' personalities and their preferences for teamwork and collaboration. Do they, for instance, prefer leadership positions? Do they rather like to be a team member? Are they the organizers, or are they the doers? Understanding these competencies ensures that the manager can manage his or her team better and get the most out of each individual.

- **Productivity:** One of the main objectives, of course, in team building is to optimize productivity. At the end of the day, a small business, or any business for that matter, has to survive. Surviving means reaching the bottom-line targets. And that can only be done by engaged people who contribute optimally to productivity. And productivity simply means that the outputs must be more than the inputs.

- **Trust and morale:** Team building has the side effect of getting people to trust each other because they share a great deal of themselves in the process. This builds mutual respect and is a great contributor to morale (Prachi, 2018).

The Process of Team Building

I won't cover specific team-building activities or techniques here. Those are to be found everywhere on the internet through a quick search. The activities that you use will depend on a number of things, including the maturity of your team, the type of business and work environment that you function in, and the specific reason why you want to do team building.

Generally speaking, team building helps to:

- Develop goals for a team
- Demonstrate how goals and other priorities are aligned
- Show how the work is to be done
- Show how the work is performing at present
- Consider the relationships among the people in the team

The process of team building is iterative, meaning that it's not linear or a one-off. It involves some steps that can be repeated as often as are required, and not all of them need to be done every time, too.

- **Identification of the problem:** As usual, like with any problem-solving exercise, clearly identifying the problem is the most important part. The emphasis should be on getting consensus. Everyone should agree on the problem, be it an organizational one, a team one, or an individual one. Here, already, one should be able to see whether the rest of the exercise should lean toward improving communication or something else (pro tip: communication is generally the issue…).

- **Identification of differences:** Here, one can do the various exercises that I alluded to earlier so that personal (and personality) differences can be highlighted. Personality profiles must be shared between members so that everyone can understand everyone else's preferences and make-up. For the facilitator, it's important to show that there are no right or wrong profiles. The major takeaway here is altered perceptions.

- **Sharing feedback:** All the members of the team should talk. Now that everyone has a better view of the other, this should be easier, even for introverts. People should now say what their opinions are and how they experience things. The concept of the Johari Window may also be applied here. A simple Johari Window test shows the level of people's self-awareness. Simply put, if you have a large Johari Window, it means that you're a relatively open book, while a small window may mean that people cannot easily fathom you. This stage requires a good facilitator because there could be outbreaks of conflict.

- **Promoting interaction:** The objective here is to promote the ability of the team members to interact with each other in a constructive manner and to avoid negative behaviors. Negative behaviors could include over-talking, attacking, avoiding, or undermining. Constructive behaviors include building bridges, encouraging participation, clarifying, and bringing in new ideas. The methodology usually involves people writing down what they plan to do to ensure constructive behavior. If this is reinforced often, it tends to stick over time. This is one of the stages that can be reactivated at short notice if the manager feels that issues have not been resolved as they relate to the identified problem.

- **Following up:** This is the last stage. The team is called together to discuss the lessons learned and to discuss the way ahead. Responsibilities are assigned as to who should follow up on specific issues identified. Dates are set for the next sessions and the expectations for those sessions are also communicated so that everyone is on the same page as to how to prepare themselves.

Effective team building is vital to ensure that the organization's culture stays healthy and that people remain engaged. It builds cooperative and supportive feelings among people involved in the team functioning. When this exercise is undertaken initially, everyone usually emerges full of confidence and motivation. This feeling rapidly dissipates in the cold light of the work environment, so management needs to undertake such actions at regular intervals so that members feel reinforced and maintain their positive behavior (*Process of Team Building*, n.d.).

Having happy and engaged people is important. But a business leader cannot afford to only be internally-focused. You also have to engage with the outside world. Networking is key to market yourself and your business and also to do some best-practice research into other business practices.

5

BUSINESS NETWORKING AND HOW IT WORKS

"Networking is an investment in your business. It takes time and when done correctly can yield great results for years to come."

—Diane Helbig

Undertaking business networking is an effective approach to marketing to develop contacts and hence sales. This is done either face-to-face or by other contact methods such as phone, email and, increasingly, social and business networking websites.

Business networking brings you closer to your potential clients or customers. Sometimes, networking might not bring clients or customers to your business, but it might open your eyes to new opportunities or more effective and less expensive methods of doing business.

Some Important Considerations

Business networking is, of course, nothing new. It's been happening forever. The exchange of information to further matters of mutual benefit, like gathering food, bartering, finding out where water is, are all examples of networking done by our forebears. It's a function of communication, and as long as we've communicated with each other there has been networking. And, because it has just about always been done with some ulterior motive in mind, it has always come down to furthering business interests, even if those interests had to do with survival.

Nowadays, whenever people get together for Chamber of Commerce meetings, go to conventions, or ask someone for introductions or recommendations, they're networking. And that has led to the adage, "It's not what you know that counts; it's whom you know." Few of us will dispute the wisdom of this.

What has changed now, though, is the advent of the internet era. We have new networking tools at our disposal. Just think about all the social media sites that link people with common interests together into chat rooms or dedicated product sites.

But, because people have become clued in to why people want to network, it has become a real skill to do it effectively. Trading business cards no longer cuts it. Neither does spamming people's email boxes. Even attending in-person functions and other things may be a waste of time if not done properly. The point is that there needs to be a strategy in your networking approach. You have to define the ends (what you want to achieve), ways (how you want to achieve it), and means (with what resources are you going to achieve it) of networking for it to be successful.

Business Networking Groups

Even though networking sounds logical and easy, many small business owners have no idea where to start. Remember that networking can be done anywhere, from the gym to family members. If you're stuck, you could consider the following possibilities, but a word of caution—don't get stuck doing all of them on a cursory basis. This will just diffuse your time and effort without bringing the best results. The best option is to deeply involve yourself in only a couple of options, to get the best return on your time investment.

- **Your local chamber of commerce:** This is often the best place to start, and the easiest. All towns have this, or some variation on the theme, and they invariably assist with training, resources, and professional development for local business owners. They often host functions that give opportunities for networking and sometimes bring in guest speakers, and even could provide mentoring opportunities at a reasonable price. The easiest way to network is to contact your local commerce department to obtain more detail.
- **SCORE:** SCORE is a non-profit business association that has provided opportunities for small business owners for over 50 years. They provide free online learning opportunities and in-person mentor relationships. SCORE is one of the most affordable

ways to network, as they're also supported by the US Small Business Administration and corporate donations.

- **Entrepreneurs' Organization:** This association has developed a community of more than 10,000 business owners around the world who share knowledge and build their business networks. They provide mentor relationships, online networks, and host global networking events. Each local chapter has a different set of offerings. Many EO members have mentioned the positive impact of this organization on their professional and personal lives.
- **Business Networking International:** This is a more transactional type of approach where members share contacts, rather than focus on community building.
- **Young Entrepreneurs Council:** This is aimed at entrepreneurs under 40. They provide professional development and networking opportunities for millennials. It's more digitally-focused, rather than in-person networking organizations.
- **American Marketing Association:** Your local AMA chapter may be a great place to form connections and learn from fellow marketers and entrepreneurs in your community.
- **Rotary Club International:** Rotary Club isn't specifically a small business group, but more of a community service and leadership development. Many successful small business owners do, however, cite their local Rotary Club as crucial to their own

business success (*The 7 Best Small Business Groups for Networking*, n.d.).

Apart from these in-person opportunities, the biggest move in the internet era has been to social media networking.

Social Networking for Business

Many social media sites are used for networking. Names that come to mind include Facebook, Instagram, LinkedIn, Twitter, Ryze, Ning, and Meetup. There are also others. Blogs are also a good way to connect with people and post messages.

Social media makes it easy to network and find contacts. It's also less stressful for people with more introverted personalities, who dread going to meetings in person. But, as with in-person meetings, business networking in any form has to have an aim in mind, or else you're just wasting your own and others' time.

Some of the dangers of using social media to network include the following:

- One bad remark or slip-up and it's out there in your whole network. So, one has to be careful about tone, language use, and your general angle of repertoire.
- Be careful not to use social media as one-way traffic for posting about yourself or your products. People may think that you're self-centered and, over time, start ignoring you.
- Social media should not be used as an alternative to face-to-face networking, but rather as an addition.

Networking must help you reach your business goals. For that to happen, you need to consider some basic networking guidelines, no matter the format of your networking.

Business Networking Tips

Some tips include:

- Be genuinely interested in getting to know others. Show this by asking questions and exhibiting great listening skills, as discussed earlier.
- Be responsive and give feedback when asked for it. Follow up on previous discussions or outstanding points.
- Cultivate trust and respect.
- Put in the time and do the research. Research who you want to meet and, once you've met people, research their backgrounds to further see how connections may be developed.
- Set clear goals about what you hope to attain.
- Once you've met someone, follow up with a call, email, or social media message.
- Don't make commitments that you can't or don't want to stick to.
- Know what you have to offer so that you can make that obvious to others right from the start. It's also a great way to get conversations going.
- Stay visible. Maintain your contacts and keep the network alive even when you don't need it. Times change.

When you attend face-to-face networking, the rules are somewhat different:

- Use the normal rules for effective communication. Turn off your cellphone, be polite, smile, and be attentive to your body language. Use active listening to show that you are engaged. Have a good, firm handshake.
- You should be prepared to answer questions about who you are and your business. Try not to make it seem like a rehearsed speech though. Better to let it flow like a normal conversation.
- Try to get actively involved by assuming or volunteering for leadership positions in your community or the forums that you are attending.
- Be prepared. Before you go to a meeting, try to find out as much as possible about the purpose, who will be there, their backgrounds, etc.
- I already said you should be clear on your goals in going to meetings, or networking in any way for that matter. This could be to get referrals, find a new career, learn better business practices, or something else, but you have to know what it is (Brinson, n.d.).

So, your people are engaged. Great. You've made a lot of contacts. Even better. But something still isn't clicking. Some days you just feel like you're floating. Like there's some disjunct between you and the business. Make no mistake, we all have our off days. But if this is a persistent feeling, you may have to consider developing your critical thinking skills. Chapter 6 provides some guidelines.

6

THE IMPORTANCE OF CRITICAL THINKING IN BUSINESS

"You only have to do a few things right in your life so long as you don't do too many things wrong."

–Warren Buffett

T he quality of your life depends on the quality of the decisions that you make which, in turn, are impacted by the quality of your critical thinking skills. And, considering that we each make on average 35,000 decisions a day, I would say it's pretty important to get a handle on the quality of those decisions!

What is Critical Thinking?

Critical thinking is a comprehensive phenomenon that has been emerging in social science over the past 2,500 years, but has only been termed such during the 20th century by the man who many consider to be the father of critical thinking, the philosopher John Dewey. Dewey also referred to the concept as "reflective thought" or "reflection."

Long before Dewey, the first documented treatise related to critical thinking is attributed to Socrates, although the concept was, of course, not known by that name then. Socrates established the importance of "seeking evidence, closely examining reasoning and assumptions, analyzing basic concepts, and tracing out implications not only of what is said but of what is done as well" (*Critical Thinking*, n.d.).

In the process, Socrates established the fact that one cannot depend upon those in "authority" to have sound knowledge and insight. He demonstrated that persons may have power and high position and still be deeply confused and irrational. He formulated the strategy of asking penetrating questions that would delve deeply into deeply-held beliefs before we accept concepts and ideas as trustworthy and worthy of emulating or following.

One could deduce from Socrates' explanation that critical thinking is closely related to evidence-based decision-making. A more complex definition is as follows, "Critical thinking is the intellectually disciplined process of actively and skillfully conceptualizing, applying, analyzing, synthesizing, and/or evaluating information gathered from, or generated by, observation, experience, reflection, reasoning, or communication, as a guide to belief and action" (Alban, n.d.).

In essence, critical thinking is about using logic, background, and education to make sure that relevant facts are established within the proper context, and that answers are sought within this context. It is, therefore, predicated on theory as well as practice.

Benefits of Good Critical Thinking Skills

People who are well-versed in critical thinking can look beyond the obvious and also consider the possible. They tend to be less swayed by cognitive dissonance (not being able to make sense of what is coming at them) and more able to think logically and rationally. It's a way to move past the limitations of irrational thinking. To a large extent, the reason for people being increasingly unable to display good critical thinking skills has to do with the surfeit of information that we're bombarded with daily. It leads to sensory overload (still wondering why you may be "floating" some days?).

Some specific ways that critical thinking can impact your life include the following:

- **To make better decisions:** I mentioned earlier that we all make thousands of decisions every day. Most of these aren't very important, like "what will I wear today?" But others may be, "what house shall I buy today?" At work, your decisions may materially impact the lives of others. So, critical thinking skills make you better able to make important decisions. There are three commonly recognized critical thinking styles that we'll cover in more detail in Chapter 9—directive, behavioral, and analytical.

- **To promote career success:** Obvious career paths where critical thinking is important include scientists, doctors, engineers, analysts, accountants, and more. Critical thinking is, however, becoming an important skill in more and more professions in the 4IR where you must:

- Systematically solve problems.
- Create innovative solutions.
- Think strategically.
- Analyze information.
- Be creative.
- Present your ideas in an easy-to-understand format.
- **To increase your happiness:** Critical thinking is part of having a high EI, as we've covered before. Therefore, people with high critical thinking skills are extremely self-aware. They know themselves and know how to express their feelings and ideas. And, because quality of life depends to a large extent on the quality of your decisions and thoughts, it means that you should be happier. It provides you with a process that you can trust, making decisions less stressful. Critical thinking also boosts your confidence when you see those around you trust your opinion, since they know it's based on facts.
- **To improve relationships:** Because critical thinking keeps you from jumping to conclusions and because it makes you more open-minded and able to also see other people's points of view, you are better able to see when others:
- Are less than honest.
- Try to take advantage of you.
- Try to manipulate you.
- **To make you a more rounded person:** Rounded individuals are considered to have fully developed personalities. They holistically embrace life. Critical thinkers are more holistic human beings. They see, sense, and feel. They don't get swept up in hysteria

and also can see through fake news. They're the
living embodiment of the quote (incorrectly
attributed to Thomas Jefferson), "An educated
citizenry is a vital requisite for our survival as a free
people" (Alban, n.d.).

How to Improve Your Critical Thinking Skills

I suppose one of the best ways to describe critical thinking
skills is the ability to connect the dots and thereby be able to
see the whole picture. In the intelligence world, critical
thinking skills are highly valued, exactly because of this ability
that it gives intelligence analysts to connect the dots and make
some sort of sense from less than optimal intelligence information that's coming at them.

So, how do you develop this skill to see the dots?

- **Clearly define the problem:** The most important
  part of decision-making and problem-solving is
  making sure that the problem is properly
  formulated. Critical thinkers spend a great deal of
  time making sure that they fully understand the
  issue that they're about to address before starting
  with the project.
- **Gather the best relevant information:** In a world
  constantly bombarded by social media fake news,
  this is becoming an increasing challenge. Critical
  thinkers only consider the best information from the
  most reliable sources and disregard the rest. They
  know that they can't afford to have their thinking
  processes clouded by peripheral "noise," hence they

focus only on what is necessary to address the specific issue or problem in front of them.

- **Apply the information and ask the correct questions:** Critical thinkers will often surround themselves with the best minds so that they can get the best possible solution to a problem. They'll analyze all the information that they've focused on with a critical eye and will use proper analytical techniques. One example is the Five Whys that we covered previously. Another could be fishbone analysis or Failure Mode Effects Analysis (FMEA). There are dozens of these techniques. The point is that these individuals have a toolbox available that they can dip into to select just the right tool for any occasion. Once they understand the "why" they ask "how."

- **Consider the consequences:** Look at what could happen because of the course of action that was selected. Because critical thinkers are big picture thinkers, they understand the issue of context and systems theory, and that everything is related to everything else. Therefore any decision taken must have downstream (unintended) consequences.

- **Explore all possibilities:** Also, consider the full spectrum of viewpoints. Examine why others are arriving at different conclusions and what their logic is. This may help you further evaluate your viewpoint objectively (Alban, n.d.).

So, it's simply a matter of drawing up these five questions in a small list that you keep handy and, as you're confronted by a decision-making or problem-solving situation, you apply these questions until it eventually becomes second nature. I've used this with great success, and you find that over time,you improvise on the list and make it unique to your own personality.

In the next chapter we'll move on to a biggy: marketing. Getting yourself and your product or service known out there in the marketplace. It need not be a complex undertaking, but it is a crucially important one. There are some businesses where the customers just keep walking in the door. Many fast food restaurants come to mind. They seem not to need to market their product, but think again. They all started somewhere. KFC wasn't KFC on day one. Neither was McDonald's. Or Wendy's. Each individual franchise might not have to market themselves. The franchisor does that. At a price of course. But for your small business it is crucial to know how to position yourself out there amongst the competition.

MARKETING CONCEPTS AND STRATEGIES

"Customer experience is the number one driver of growth in 2021 and beyond. This has been happening for a while, but 2020 really accelerated trends in digital transformation and buyer-seller relationships and there is no going back."

–Yamini Ramgan

You may have quality goods and services to offer, but knowing how to tell the world about them and attract potential customers is another ball game. Marketing is a skill every successful business leader of this century has used. It's a skill that can be learned and used to fit a business brand.

The obvious question, then, is–exactly what is marketing?

What is Marketing?

Marketing relates to the actions undertaken by a business to make potential consumers aware of their products or services through a variety of channels and messages. It aims to provide value for customers, present and future, through content. The long-term goal is to convince the target audience of the product or service's value, to strengthen brand value, and of course, ultimately lead to more sales.

Marketing is, of course, as old as the ages. In times gone by, one could find merchandisers flashing their wares at stalls in small markets all over the world. That was nothing but marketing. Eventually, this moved onto the print media in about the 1800s. Modern marketing arose in the 1950s, when other marketing media started appearing, like TV and later the internet. This resulted in multiple media becoming available for marketers. The advent of social media heralded in yet another dimension.

The Purpose of Marketing

The purpose of marketing is to get people interested in your offering, be it a product or a service. It's as simple as that. And as complicated. Because to do that, you have to conduct market research, analyze the results, and understand your target customer's interests and wants. Research can be done by doing focus groups, sending out surveys, or by studying online shopping habits.

Marketing is relevant to all sides of a business, including product development, distribution methods, sales, and advertising.

An important part of conveying your message to customers is to understand the concept of signal value and real value. Real value is the real value that you can deliver to your customer through your product (the same applies to a service, but let's stick to a physical product for the sake of simplicity). Signal value is the underlying "other" benefits that the customer associates with that product. It may sometimes be difficult to express in words or to quantify in monetary terms.

Let us use the example of cars. A Mercedes is generally regarded as a high-quality product, but there are many high-quality cars out there. However, that star on the bonnet has some inherent signal value that a customer is willing to pay more for. A Kia, as an example, is nowadays just as high quality as a Mercedes. It has equally good build characteristics, yet people are prepared to pay thousands more for some signal value attached to that brand. That star. Maybe it's the prestige value. The safety factor. Whatever. For every person, it'll be difficult and yet others may find it hard to say exactly why they value that brand so highly.

This is an important concept to keep in mind when you develop your marketing plan, because you can go a long way by just promoting signal value. In the end, though, customers will always fall back onto the real value of something. Signal value by itself doesn't deliver value.

Types of Marketing

There are several types of marketing strategies that may be used. Your market research should show you which of these would be best suited to your purpose:

- **Print marketing:** Businesses keep on using newspapers and other printed media for marketing. Relatively speaking, this is now a more expensive form of marketing than many other electronic options. Other forms of print marketing include posters, flyers, brochures, business cards, etc.
- **Internet marketing:** Having a website on the internet is nowadays almost indispensable if you want to conduct proper marketing. It's also required to properly use the approaches that we'll discuss next. A website helps customers get a better overview of who you are and what you offer. It also lends your business some gravitas if you have a properly designed website in a world flooded with less than perfect examples.
- **Search engine optimization (SEO):** To use your website properly, you need to optimize the content on your site so that it appears close to the top in search engine results. If your side is SEO-optimized, that means that most searches for a particular product or service will have you listed in the first five results, and that even "peripheral" searches, i.e. searches for something that isn't exactly what you provide but is perhaps a substitute product or service, will also find you.
- **Search engine marketing:** Somewhat different from SEO, this means that an advertiser can pay a publisher when the ad that is placed on their website is clicked–so-called "pay-per-click."
- **Blog marketing:** Writing blogs has become a big business, and all decent websites have blogs

associated with their product or service. It's become a fine art to write blogs that create general interest in the industry that you have a business in, versus doing "harder" marketing for your specific business, something which is sometimes a bit off-putting to customers.

- **Social media marketing:** Facebook, Instagram, Twitter, LinkedIn, and other social networks are fast surpassing other channels of marketing in both amount of use and also success rates.
- **Video marketing:** This can be a stand-alone function, but is often used in conjunction with the channels mentioned above. So, if you have a website, as one example, it's a good idea to have it SEO optimized, pay search engines to list your business, have links to your social media sites on it, have blogs on it, and have videos embedded in your content.

But wait! Isn't this more advertising than marketing?

Marketing and Advertising

In a sense, you're right. The saying goes that if marketing is a cake, advertising is one slice of that cake.

Marketing involves matters like research, products and how they're distributed, approaches to getting products in front of customers, customer support, and how the public is engaged, i.e. public relations. Marketing is required during a business' lifecycle, and can employ various teams, platforms, and social media channels to identify the audience and communicate with them in the ultimate pursuit of building brand loyalty over time.

So, if your marketing campaign is about creating brand awareness about product X, your advertising campaign will be, as an example, to do it on the various social media platforms mentioned above. And/or to send out flyers. And/or to develop a video. Advertising, therefore, is seen as a component of marketing (Forsey, 2021).

So much, then, for marketing and advertising. But where do sales fit into all of this?

What are Sales?

As we indicated above, marketing relates to all activities that get people interested in your business and in what you have to offer. Marketing departments run strategies to make people aware of and attract them to the business's product or service and brand.

Sales, on the other hand, are all activities that end in the sale of goods and services. Salespeople manage relationships with potential clients (prospects) and provide a solution for prospects that eventually leads to a sale.

Another difference is that marketing focuses on the general public or larger groups of people, while sales targets smaller groups of people or subsets of the general public.

Yet another difference is that the marketing plan describes what the product is, who the customers typically are, and where it should be sold. These are known as the 4Ps of marketing, and we'll get to them later. The plan determines the goals to be achieved, the channels to be used, and the budget for that specific campaign.

Sales plans, on the other hand, include details about the sales process, the team to be involved, the target market in detail, and sub-goals, or objectives.

Sales are also more focused on the short-term than marketing, as they focus on hitting quotas and sales volumes that are normally tracked over months. The difference between the two concepts can also be seen in the tools of their respective "trades."

Marketing tools include:

- Conversion Rate Optimization (CRO).
- Search engine optimization (SEO).
- Project management tools like MS Project or Asana.
- Data reporting software.
- Content creation tools like SurveyMonkey, Snappa,Wideo,Venngage, Meme Generator, GameFroot, NoNotes, and many others.

Sales tools could include:

- Meeting apps.
- Document tools.
- Invoicing software.
- Email management tools.
- Inventory and order management software like Unicommerce, Trello, Shipfusion, or Caspio (Hart, 2019).

Marketing Concepts

Not to confuse matters, but apart from what we've discussed till now, it's also important to understand that, within a holistic marketing strategy, there needs to be included the five different concepts of marketing:

- The Production Concept
- The Product Concept
- The Selling Concept
- The Marketing Concept
- The Societal Marketing Concept

Not all of these may be equally relevant to your business, but you need to use them all as a sort of prism through which your marketing strategy is developed. Some may be more relevant than others.

The following is a definition of a marketing concept as provided by Robert Katai, a marketing strategist, "A strategy that companies and marketing agencies design and implement in order to satisfy customers' needs, maximize profits, satisfy customer needs, and beat the competitors or outperform them" (Wilson, 2020). Let's look at each in a bit more detail.

The Production Concept

The production concept is about producing high volume, low cost output. By implication, it also means that the output quality may not be the best. This can be a way to penetrate the market if that market is still immature or the product is very new and in high demand. It can be a dangerous approach to follow if customers are keen on quality, as they mostly are nowadays.

In days gone by it was generally assumed that there were only two strategies for competing in a marketplace: you were either the low-cost, low-quality producer or the high-cost, high-quality producer. That approach is slowly going out the door as customers increasingly want high quality but at lower prices. They're becoming more attuned to the product concept.

The Product Concept

The product concept focuses more on the customer, and it says that customers are more interested in products that offer quality, performance, or innovative features. Brand loyalty is closely tied to options of products, the quality of those products, and the benefits customers get from the product and the business they invest in. Apple products are good examples of this.

In this concept, businesses will concentrate on making higher quality products and improving them over time.

The Selling Concept

The selling concept has as its essence the fact that you have to convince people to buy products that they don't want. You need to be good at finding potential customers and emotionally selling them on the benefits of your "not needed product."

This concept puts a lot of power into the hands of a business that has a plan to effectively stimulate more buying with its potential customers. We often see this ploy used when a business has too much capacity or output and has to get rid of what they make rather than target the market's needs.

The Marketing Concept

The marketing concept is the concept of competition. It's an approach that believes that the success of a business depends on marketing efforts that deliver a better value proposition than its competitors.

Here the needs and wants of the target market are prioritized, in the process attempting to deliver better value than the competition. Through marketing, you attempt to have customers select you rather than a competitor product. Competitive advantage is key!

The marketing concept has evolved into a fifth and more refined company marketing orientation: the societal marketing concept.

The Societal Marketing Concept

The societal marketing concept is most applicable today in the modern marketplace. This concept follows an approach that we need to give back to society in whatever we produce or consume. It's strongly premised on the idea of Corporate Social Responsibility (CSR).

This orientation arose as some questioned whether marketing and businesses are addressing the massive problems society has, like environmental deterioration, resource shortages, population growth, poverty, obesity, and social disruption.

All of these marketing concept mindsets can help you achieve organizational goals depending on whether you understand the needs and wants of your target market while delivering quality products people prefer (Hatch, 2020).

The 4 Ps of Marketing

The 4 Ps of marketing were introduced in the 1960 textbook *Basic Marketing: A Managerial Approach,* written by Jerome McCarthy. This so-called marketing mix has since provided a standard approach to marketing programs for more than 50 years.

The 4 Ps of marketing–product, price, place, and promotion–is a tool used to help brands understand what elements must be combined in order to meet their marketing goals and objectives.

Product

A product is something that is meant to satisfy the needs and/or wants of a target audience. Needs and wants are not the same things, but for the sake of brevity, we'll continue using the term needs (needs are must-haves; wants are nice-to-haves). It can be tangible, like a car or computer, or a service, like cleaning, security, or maintenance.

Marketers must be clear about what their products stand for and about what differentiates them from the competition. In getting to understand this, some key questions that they need to be able to answer include:

- What do customers want from this product or service to satisfy their needs?

- What features does it need to have to satisfy customer needs?
- Where and in which ways will the customer use it?
- What will the customer experience be?

Price

Once the product or service has been determined, it needs to be priced. Price includes the monetary value as well as the time and effort that the customer needs to spend to acquire something. The product and the brand will fail if the price is too high or low. Too high and the customer will think it unreasonable for that market segment. Too low and the customer might think it doesn't add enough value (remember real and signal value).

Questions that the market must have answers to include:

- What is the value (real and signal) to the buyer?
- How does it compare to competitors?

Other important considerations include looking at the whole buyer experience cyle:

- **Purchase:** How quickly can the product be found and how secure is the transactional environment?
- **Delivery:** How easy is to get the product delivered and how difficult or easy is its installation?
- **Use:** Are there special training requirements for the use of the product and to what degree is it over- or under specified?
- **Supplements:** Can the product operate on its on or

do you need other products to make it work and how much effort will be involved in doing that?

- **Maintenance:** Does the product require maintenance from outside and if so how easy and expensive is it to arrange?
- **Disposal:** How easy is the product to dispose of and does it create waste materials? How costly is the process of disposal?

Blue Ocean Strategy has developed an interesting approach to establish what they call the price corridor of the target mass. To first establish the price corridor, they determine whether the product/service has a different form but performs the same function. In other words, are there alternatives? On the other side of the spectrum, they look at whether the product/service may have a different form and function, but with the same objective in mind.

An example of the first approach is children eating at school. They can either have packed meals from home or eat at the cafeteria. It's the same function but comes in different forms.

An example of the second approach would be travel to a certain destination. The objective is the same–to arrive at the destination. But the form and function of reaching it might be different–traveling by car or aircraft.

Once this price corridor has been established, ranging from same form products or services on the one side through to different form but same function products/service in the middle, and finally to different form and function but with the same objective on the other side of the spectrum, you then move on to the second step–determining how high a price to set within that corridor without inviting competition in from competing products or services. To do this, they consider three questions:

- Does the product or service have a high level of legal and resource protection? In other words, it may be difficult to imitate. This allows you to do upper-level pricing.
- Does the product or service have some degree of legal and resource protection? This will allow you to do mid-level pricing.
- Does the product or service have a low level of legal and resource protection? This results in you having to enter the market at a lower level.

Place

The internet age brings new challenges when it comes to reaching customers. But, whether it is digital marketing or otherwise, marketing means putting in front of the customer the right product, at the right place, and at the right time.

To do this effectively the marketer needs to answer the following:

- Where do my target customers shop?
- What devices do they use to shop with, if it's digital? PC or mobile?
- Do they shop online or in real shops for the same products?
- How do they engage on social media?

Promotion

This one is about communications, about how to make your audience aware of your product. The communication channels could include public relations, advertising, direct marketing, email marketing, social media marketing, or sales promotions.

Some questions to consider include:

- How to reach the target audience?
- Where to send the messages to the target audience?
- How does the competition do it and what can you learn from it?
- When are the best times to do promotion?

Using the 4 Ps

Together, as alluded to before, the 4 Ps comprise the so-called marketing mix. They all have to feature in your marketing strategy to a greater or lesser degree, together with consideration of the 7 Cs that we'll get to in the next section. Specific steps to follow include:

- Select the product or service for analysis.
- Consider it in line with the 4 Ps to formulate a marketing mix.

Once you've done that, do a trial run to see how it could work from a customer's point of view. To do that, you should ask:

- Will it satisfy their needs?

- Will the price be seen as reasonable?
- Will they know where to find it?
- Have you put in place the proper communications mechanisms to get to your target audience?

You should continue to do this regularly to ensure that your marketing mix for a specific product or service always remains fresh and aligned to best practice and to what works within that specific time and market (Manthei, 2017).

The 7 Cs of Marketing

The 4 Ps form the basis of your marketing strategy. To expand on that, and to make sure that you cover all your bases, you should also consider the 7 Cs.

Customer

It's vital that the business understands and knows its target customers very well. You cannot invest enough time and energy into this. The customer must be seen as a living person, not just some amorphous target market out there. And every person's needs change over time, so you need to stay attuned to changes in the customer's needs. These changes can be because of the introduction of new competitor products, new substitute products, or new demands created by changes in the environment.

Consistency

Marketing communications must remain consistent to prevent customers from being confused. If customers perceive different messages coming from a business regarding the same product or service offering, they'll lose trust in the offering and the business. Nobody likes inconsistency. It impacts trust, whether in a business relationship or a personal one. Your value proposition should stay consistent.

Creativity

The 4IR era has resulted in an explosion of creativity on the internet. This affects how products and services are presented, along with the visual attractiveness offered. Customers increasingly demand that offerings be presented to them in a creative fashion that speaks to the exigencies of the era that they live in. As an example, in an era plagued by pandemics, natural remedies that are marketed as increasing a person's natural resistance to infections may have a better hit rate than in other circumstances.

Culture

Cultural influences are becoming very important for marketing campaigns. As is the influence of "subcultures" like the LBGTQ movement, BLM, etc. Marketers have to be increasingly aware of how the rise of these movements impacts their market segmentation and product offerings. A one-size-fits-all approach hasn't worked for a long time and is increasingly likely to be unsuccessful in the future.

Communication

People prefer to be communicated with rather than to be

marketed to. They may know what's actually happening, but a buyer-savvy population increasingly resents hard marketing efforts. This is why a popular approach nowadays is to hide the marketing message under the guise of "education." By educating the target market about a certain topic, the marketing message gets across, sometimes subtly, other times not so subtly. This is why one often sees internet articles on subjects containing links to offerings that are related, but are only activated by the potential customer themselves, thereby not being too in their face.

Change

Although the marketing message regarding a certain offering should remain stable, as should the value proposition, the way that it gets conveyed to the target market can and should change regularly. Customers like to see freshness in the approach that a business uses to get their message across. Nothing is so boring than to see the same product being advertised in the same format year in and year out. That gives an immediate opening to your competitors.

Channel

We covered this in some detail before, but it's important to understand the transformational impact of the internet on marketing. Similarly with social media, which is expanding by the day.

So, in the end, everything comes down to developing your marketing strategy.

Developing Your Marketing Strategy

Everything that we've discussed till now leads up to and should feed into the development of your marketing strategy. Your marketing strategy is, of course, a sub-strategy to your overall business strategy. You can't even begin to develop your marketing strategy if your business strategy isn't in place. Your marketing strategy is closely aligned with your business strategy and should dovetail with it closely concerning:

- Describing your business and the products or services.
- Explaining the positioning of your products or services in the market.
- The profiles of your customers and your competitors.
- The tactics that you'll use.
- The marketing plan (how the tactics will be implemented).

A marketing strategy is long-term, maybe even as long as five to ten years into the future, aligned with your business's vision. Your marketing plan is normally one year, aligned with your annual budget.

To develop a successful marketing strategy, you need to consider the following elements:

- **The business goals:** By now you should have developed them, either through a BSC approach as we explained earlier or otherwise. The marketing strategy should be aligned to the achievement of your business goals or why do marketing at all? Some of your relevant business goals that you've developed may include increasing awareness of your products or services in a specific target market or reaching a new customer market segment.

- **The marketing goals:** These should now dovetail with your business goals. So, this could mean market penetration to sell more to existing clients or market development where you sell existing products to new client markets. These goals should be formulated according to the SMART principles that we elaborated on earlier in the book.

- **Market research:** The market needs to be researched in terms of specific elements that you'll determine beforehand, but could include growth, size, social trends, demographics, age, gender, spending power, etc.

- **Customer profiling:** Based upon your market research, you will now develop a profile of the customers that you'll pursue. This will reveal things like their buying patterns and where they buy.

- **Competitor profiling:** You should be able to identify your major competitor's pricing structures, marketing approaches, products, and supply chains. You need to know this to develop your competitive advantage that will differentiate your offerings from your competitors.

- **Strategy development:** To support your marketing goals, you should now list your target markets and devise ways to attract them. An example could be to increase people's awareness of your restaurant. The strategies could be to increase your presence on social media by posting updates on Facebook and Instagram every week, advertising in the local newspaper, and by offering discounts to students from the local university.

- **Making sure that you have covered the 4 Ps and the 7 Cs:** If you run your strategy against the 4 Ps and 7 Cs, you're more likely to get a robust strategy that will lead to business success.
- **Test the strategy:** Run some mini-scenarios to test the veracity of your strategy. Implement some elements that are cheap and see what the feedback is. Sit down with your team and consider tweaking it until it works. You don't have to implement everything overnight. In fact, it's wise to do so incrementally, learning as you go (*Develop a Marketing Strategy*, 2021).

As an interesting aside on matters related to marketing strategy—in 2021, HubSpot's *Not Another State of Marketing Report* found that marketing strategy is changing. The priority platform for companies to use is social media, which in turn would suggest that "conversational marketing" and a more personalized approach are now becoming preferred. Brand awareness is becoming more important (the #3 overall marketing priority) and it has even surpassed sales as a goal for running campaigns. The #1 goal remains "generating more leads," while "increasing customer satisfaction" comes in at #2 (HubSpot, 2021).

So, you have strategized. You have planned. You have motivated. You have built your team. Business is booming. Yet, suddenly you notice a decrease in sales. Fewer feet entering the shop, or less internet orders. This may not be so noticeable over the short term. But over the months, you grow increasingly concerned, because this is definitely not a one-off. This is a trend! Maybe it's due to some dishonesty in the business? Something done by your or your staff? Let's consider what we mean when we talk about honesty in the business.

8

HONESTY IN BUSINESS

"Character cannot be developed in ease and quiet. Only through experience of trial and suffering can the soul be strengthened, ambition inspired and success achieved."
–Helen Keller

Every leader should know that honesty is about more than doing business. It creates strong bonds of friendship, something that goods or services, no matter the quality, cannot forge. Honesty is essential for a business because it (a) establishes the type of culture that you want to develop in your business, (b) allows for consistent work behavior because everyone knows the rules and how to toe the line, as well as the penalties for not doing so, and (c) builds trust in customers and subsequent buyer loyalty.

Honesty and ethics, when applied to business, might not buy you friends in the short term, but people will learn to trust your brand because they feel assured of the quality of goods or services. Conversely, a lack of trust as a result of dishonesty can cost the business money and customers.

How honest are we? Well, a University of Massachusetts study found that 60% of people lie at least once during a ten-minute conversation (Silva, 2017). In fact, it was found that many tell two to three lies during that period! And in the business world, there's a general attitude of "well, everyone tells white lies," as if that makes the whole matter more acceptable. But where does the border between "white lies" and "big lies" start and stop? And what about my definition of "white lies" versus yours?

You see, once you venture down this road, it rapidly becomes a self-defeating spiral leading to a bad ending. And where do concepts like ethics and integrity come into play? We'll cover those in the next sections.

The Price of Dishonesty

There are several things being dishonest–yourself or your employees–can do to hurt your business:

- **It can affect your present customer base:** Once someone feels that they have been cheated by a business, real or perceived, they're not likely to turn into repeat customers. And remember the importance of perceptions. What you do may not amount to being dishonest, but the customer may perceive it as such. That's why it is so important to be transparent in everything you do when it comes to customer interaction.
- **It can impact your ability to attract new**

customers: With the advent of social media, there's no way that dishonesty in business stays hidden for long. There are too many social groups that speak to each other in the B2B and B2C chat groups. Once your reputation becomes tainted, it becomes an uphill battle to woo new customers or investors.

- **It erodes internal business trust:** We touched on this before, but if you want to be seen as a leader, it means that you have to be trusted. Once your employees start getting a feeling that you may not always be honest in your dealings or conversations with them, it becomes a difficult situation to recover from. That in turn, will lead to your employees acting dishonestly because you've shown that honesty is not a requirement of this business! From there on, it's a slippery slope to anonymity.

- **Dishonesty affects you at a cellular level:** Being dishonest, especially when it becomes a way of life, triggers a stress response. It prevents you from staying in the moment and makes you less intelligent during that conversation or activity that you're undertaking. This is because, when stress hormones are released, they activate our "fight or flight" response, which means that resources are directed away from the neocortex of the brain, which handles all high-level, logical thinking. And being less intelligent at any time in business is not a good idea.

The Rewards of Being Honest

Conversely, the benefits of being honest in business almost speak for themselves:

- **It builds a solid reputation in the industry:** More than 80% of consumers investigate companies online before doing business with them or do some other form of B2B or C2B checks (like on social media). An honest reputation can be a self-fulfilling prophecy that creates a domino effect to attract more customers. Read the product descriptions of, for example,. health products on Amazon and Walmart websites. They all try to outdo each other to convince customers how honest and reliable they are. At the same time, a high premium is put on customer reviews that also highlight their trustworthiness when it comes to their products.
- **It promotes customer and employee loyalty:** If your employees see that you're honest in your dealings with customers, it will encourage them to do the same. So, as an example, if you made a mistake with invoicing a customer and you go back to the customer to apologize, even before the customer has noticed it, it sends a powerful message about your integrity as a business person to both the customer and your staff. It also firmly establishes you as a role model in your industry and among your staff.
- **It's personally rewarding:** We all know the difference between right and wrong, although we

may not all always admit to it. So, no matter how difficult it might be, being honest about your personal and/or business failings will be appreciated by customers in the long run. In a dog-eat-dog business world, your honesty will be refreshing. Because so many people lie without thinking about it, your honesty will stand out.

- **It improves your mental well-being:** Being honest creates less stress and, in fact, has the opposite effect–it releases feel-good endorphins that positively impact your levels of self-confidence which in turn will have a positive effect on your customers and your employees–a win-win all around! (Silva, 2017).

Being honest always will let your business flourish. But how is this related to integrity?

Integrity and its Worth

Integrity and honesty are closely related, but they're not the same thing. A person can be honest but lack integrity. However, you cannot have integrity without being honest. Let me explain.

Integrity means choosing the course of conduct that is correct out of a variety of options, then acting consistently with that choice, and lastly, being open and transparent about the choice and the reasons for it. This is why integrity is often associated with trustworthiness, commitment, and moral reflection.

So, the difference? One could be entirely honest about a viewpoint without having engaged in the reflection and thought on the matter that integrity requires. This may not be so important in mundane matters, but could be crucial when it comes to important business considerations.

Let me explain further by way of a practical example: in your strategic planning session for marketing, you might make a statement like "All our customers read the local newspaper." You may make that in all honesty because that is what you believe, but at that moment you lack integrity because you've not determined whether the statement is correct. In other words, compared to a range of options, like "some of our customers," "a few of our customers," "most of our customers," you have chosen "all" without ascertaining whether that is the correct choice. If you had clarified my statement by saying "based on company X's market survey done last week" it may have been closer to being a statement of integrity.

So, in this case, you would have failed the integrity test, not because you weren't honest, and not because your actions were inconsistent with your beliefs, but because you had not done the hard work to find out whether what you believed was right or wrong (Thomas, n.d.).

Be careful, therefore, when you develop your business's values to make sure that everyone understands what integrity means. It's so easy when developing values to always put integrity first and foremost without understanding the deeper meaning.

Let's look at some characteristics of integrity:

- **It's a true mark of leadership:** High-integrity leaders always err on the side of fairness. A fair process is first and foremost in your mind when dealing with employees and customers. It means you engage with people fairly and decently, you explain your actions precisely, and you set your expectations clearly. Integrity is a state of mind and is not situation-dependent, meaning you cannot decide when you want to show high integrity.

- **Leaders never compromise their integrity by cheating:** Oh, history is replete with examples of people and organizations who "won" without showing high levels of integrity. But it somehow always comes back to haunt them. Some American presidents come to mind. And what about a company like Enron? For years, Enron was upheld as a shining light, an example to be emulated by other companies. Unfortunately, as was eventually shown, Enron's success was founded on lies and its leaders lacked integrity.

- **Integrity means doing the right thing always:** Integrity is doing the right thing because it is the right thing. If there are negative consequences attached to it, then so be it. Remember, we said that a leader always remains accountable. Integrity also means keeping your promises (Tracy, 2017).

Ok, so now we have a good handle on both honesty and integrity. Both are required in business, and not only required but are essential. So then, what about ethics?

Ethics Versus Integrity

There's a close correlation between ethics and integrity, yet they're not the same. All professions have ethics, normally given as a set of rules to avoid getting into problems. Integrity is more personal and, as we have shown, is about being fair and honest in one's dealings with others.

Almost all organizations have a code of ethics. This allows employees to do their work directed by some moral principles. It's normally given to show a high standard of professionalism for the business and to ensure the protection of employees, the business, and the customer.

Professions that typically attach a great deal of value to a code of ethics are counselors, doctors, banks, civil servants, and the like. Ethics may therefore be defined as the regulations and rules that allow the person to do their work aligned to moral principles whereas integrity is about being honest and fair.

Another difference is that ethics are more externally focused whereas integrity is internal. Integrity is a choice about whether you want to follow such an approach in life, whereas ethics are not–if you're part of a business that has a code of ethics you have no choice in the matter. It stands to reason, as a result, that ethics can be imposed but integrity cannot (*Difference Between Ethics and Integrity*, 2015).

Honesty, integrity, and ethics are therefore clear *sine qua nons* for business success in the 21st century. They don't mean that you won't face problems as a business leader. But they do give you a better foundation with which to handle such problems.

But speaking of handling problems...

9

HOW TO TACKLE PROBLEMS

"There are no secrets to success. It is the result of preparation, hard work and learning from failure."
  –Colin Powell

Successful business leaders are problem solvers. Problems will always arise in business. Problem-solving, as a skill, helps you, the business leader, evaluate the problem, find out why an issue is happening, and how to resolve that issue with a tailored-made solution to your need.

While looking for solutions to their problems, business leaders look at their environment or society and identify the problems there and work toward solving them. If you want to be a thought leader in our age and time, you have to provide solutions.

Decision-Making Styles

Before we go into the mechanics of problem-solving, we have to understand how people's decision-making abilities function. If you want to minimize errors and make sure that you consistently make good decisions—related to solving problems or otherwise—it's important that you understand the basic styles that underpin how all of us make decisions. You should also get a feel for your preferred style.

Why is this important? Well, to quote just one stat—research done by Bain & Co. reveals that there's a 95% correlation between strong financial performance and companies that value effective decision-making. Good enough for you?

There are three decision-making styles. Most of us use a hybrid a hybrid between them, but one of the styles will dominate:

- **Analytical:** The decision-maker relies on data and facts. The basic assumption is that he or she is a rational person and always has perfect information available or on call at short notice. Many leaders, if not most, tend to think that they make decisions in this way, although this is not borne out by empirical evidence, as research estimates that US companies, despite their best intentions, use analytical approaches less than 20% of the time. As a result, there's always room for uncertainty in the answers arrived at using this approach.
- **Directive:** The decision-maker makes decisions based on their knowledge, background, and

experience. This is a somewhat subjective and autocratic approach because the inputs of team members aren't solicited in the process. Or, at least, not to the extent that they can be included or considered. This may, over time, result in team members feeling isolated and not being part of the problem-solving apparatus. The advantage, of course, is that decisions can be taken much faster this way. The downside, apart from the impact on morale, is that nobody has perfect information or capabilities, so the decisions made in this way will often be of sub-optimal quality.

- **Behavioral:** This is the opposite of directive. Inclusivity is the name of the game. The decision-maker tries to involve as many people as possible in the process. The result, generally, is a much happier team and the decisions arrived at should normally also be of a higher quality. The downside is, of course, the amount of time that this takes, which, depending on the type of business environment you find yourself in, may be a bit self-defeating, i.e. you may get an optimal solution but too late to be of use (Onley, 2019).

Your leadership style will also largely influence your approach to decision-making. If you're autocratic, you're likely to follow a directive style. If you're democratic, your decision-making style will probably be behavioral in nature. And, if you're a situational leader, it could be analytical. But, as I said, you'll never be just one exact style.

If you now understand your natural tendency towards making decisions, let's look at a specific problem-solving approach that can be usefully employed in business.

The Six-Step Problem-Solving Approach

The Six Steps

This process is a variation of the so-called Deming Wheel developed by W. Edwards Deming in the 1950s. He suggested a continuous improvement approach, like this one, that was called the PDCA cycle—Plan, Do, Check, and Act. The PDCA cycle has since been taken up in many problem-solving and process improvement philosophies, amongst others, as a cornerstone of Total Quality Management (TQM) and Toyota's Production System, now more commonly known as lean manufacturing.

The six steps followed here are:

- Define the issue or problem at stake.
- Determine the root cause(s).
- Develop alternatives.
- Select an optimal solution.
- Implement the solution
- Evaluate the result or outcome.

Because it's a continuous improvement process, the objective is to get to the optimal solution through a process of evolution. There are a number of advantages to using this approach.

Advantages of Six-Step Problem Solving

This approach provides the following advantages:

- **Ease:** It provides for a relatively easy process.
- **Focus:** It keeps the problem-solving group focused on the issue so that their attention isn't diffused.
- **Consensus:** It's a helpful approach to reach consensus around the issue at stake.
- **Consistency:** Everyone understands the problem-solving approach.
- **Objectivity:** Because there's a strong reliance on data, it prevents bias.
- **Collaboration:** It promotes collaboration and teamwork in the drive to find a solution.
- **Eliminates confusion:** Because one common technique is used, it prevents confusion.
- **Justification:** It provides a platform to be able to justify the results of the problem-solving exercise by showing the methodology followed.

The steps in this approach are repeatable, meaning the team can go back at any stage to a previous step, but the whole cycle must be followed in sequence from the beginning to the end. We now look at each step in somewhat more detail.

Step One: Define the Problem

I mentioned before that problem identification is the most important part of problem-solving. If you identify the wrong problem, or don't understand it correctly, you can create a whole lot of grief for you and your team downstream with wasted time and effort. Even worse, you may come up with a "solution" that can have very negative unintended consequences when implemented.

During this diagnostic stage, it is, therefore, fine to constantly go back and refine your problem definition. There's no real guideline for how it should be formulated. It could be done in one sentence, a paragraph, or a page. It all depends on the complexity of the issue that's being addressed and what's needed to make sure that everyone is 100% on board regarding the details of the problem to be solved. All the symptoms of the problem need to be identified at this stage, because together they add up to clarify the problem definition.

The group may use various techniques to properly define the problem including brainstorming, interviewing, and questionnaires. Take your time to do this step properly, even if it takes days or weeks. Of course, the nature or urgency of the problem to be solved may force you to take certain shortcuts as far as time is concerned, but try not to do this if you can.

Step Two: Determine the Root Cause(s) of the Problem

Root cause analysis can be done through the use of a variety of techniques like fishbone diagrams (Ishikawa diagrams), Pareto analysis, affinity diagrams, the 5 Whys, Failure Mode Effects Analysis (FMEA), and others.

Any technique may be used to ensure that the root cause of the problem is identified. Once again, depending on the nature of the problem, there may be several root causes. And the more complicated the system is that's being investigated, the more likely this is to be the case. Doing this is also a good way of educating your people about the various problem-solving techniques and how they work.

After completing this stage, the team should be directed to go back to the problem to see whether it should still be formulated as it is.

Step Three: Develop Alternative Solutions

Step three is more about eliminating options than it is about finding an optimal solution. To prevent groupthink, the team should be encouraged to come up with as many possible solutions as they can think of. They need to brainstorm as many solutions as possible, even if some of them are really blue sky or outlandish.

Each potential solution should be evaluated in terms of how it relates to the problem and its symptoms. If a solution is clearly not suited it should be discarded, but only after having been considered carefully. Some options may perhaps be merged to provide a more robust solution.

This is a time of free and innovative thinking. This step is not about finding the correct solution. That happens in step four.

Step Four: Select a Solution

Here all the potential solutions are evaluated and compared and the best option is selected. To do this effectively usually involves two questions:

1. **Which solution is optimal, or then, most feasible?** This

is decided by running the shortlist of solutions past the following checklist:

- Can it be implemented within an acceptable time frame?
- How does it compare in terms of cost-effectiveness, reliability, and realism?
- Will it impact our use of resources positively?
- Is it flexible and adaptable over time?
- What risks are involved in adopting the solution?
- What are the overall benefits of the solution?

2. Which solution will be supported most by those who have to implement it? The group may come up with what they think is a good solution, but if the users or implementers of the solution are someone else, it may perhaps not be acceptable to them. It may seem too unrealistic or complex to implement. So, coming up with the best solution on the planet serves no purpose if it's not going to be implemented.

Step Five: Implement the Solution

After step four and before step five the group decides what technical implementation approach to follow. It'll normally be in the form of a project plan, utilizing tools like Gantt charts, MS Project, Asana, or one of the many other project management tools that exist.

Then, once the solution as decided in step four has been selected and the project management approach decided on, the initial part of the project planning happens, during which the team decides on:

- Who the project manager will be. By then the project sponsor should be well established.
- Who else may need to be involved in the team during the project. Often, external expertise is required.
- The project timelines with milestones for specific deliverables.
- The actions that need to be taken before and during solution implementation.

Step Six: Evaluate the Outcome

We now get to the Check and Act stages of Deming's cycle. The success of the project depends on how well the team monitors its implementation and the results of such implementation on the original problem and/or the root causes. This involves, inter alia, making sure that milestones are achieved, that there are no cost overruns, and that all necessary tasks are completed.

To do this effectively there has to be a process that ensures that:

- Data is collected in the proper formats and quantities.
- Reporting mechanisms are in place, i.e. who reports what and by when.
- Regular updates are received by the team from the project manager.
- Protocols are in place to allow for the regular interrogation of results so that the team can collectively ensure that an optimal result is obtained.

Remember that this is an iterative process. So, during step six, the team must decide whether they're on track or whether they need to return to one of the previous steps to redo the work there. Maybe the solution decided on wasn't the best, so then they go back to step four.

Once the solution is deemed acceptable and goes live, the project team must continually monitor progress to ensure that everything stays on track, in the process being willing to at any stage return to the six-step process for an intervention should it be required (*The Six Step Problem Solving Model*, n.d.).

A final word on decision-making and problem-solving: the approach suggested here is a generic one that works well, but in practice, one finds that, after having used it for a couple of rounds, organizations tend to adapt it to their style and business environment. There's nothing wrong with that.

The list of specific tools or techniques that I listed here is far from exhaustive. It's your duty as the leader of the business to continually research the latest problem-solving trends and techniques. As you can see from the tools that I suggested, these are typically of either a quantitative or qualitative nature, or a combination of both. Some work better for some types of interventions than for others. As the leader, you should have at least some sort of idea as to how most of them work, so that you can have a set of tools readily available that you can suggest to the team. Even if you don't know how they work in detail, it's good to know which tools are relevant in what step. The details of the workings can be fleshed out together by you and the team, but it's your responsibility to be able to kick off the conversation by making some recommendations as to what to use, at least.

In the next chapter, we'll take a look at time management.

Whether you're solving a problem or just having an ordinary day at work, time is the one resource that you cannot replenish (no matter how good your problem-solving skills). Better to make sure that you get a handle on managing it properly right from the start.

10

BEING PRODUCTIVE WITH TIME

"Time is more valuable than money. You can get more money, but you cannot get more time."

—Jim Rohn

Working in a time-productive way enables you to consider how the work can be done more effectively and efficiently, with the result that more value can be added to the organization and its outputs. A business leader must spend the majority of their time with their team, or else it is time for them to reevaluate their priorities.

Goal setting and prioritization are important components for leadership, just as planning and the ability to make decisions are. Time management is deciding which priorities take precedence. Time is the biggest currency in the world. If managed properly, it can foster business growth and assure success and immeasurable wealth

The thing to do is to organize your tasks and learn to use

your time more effectively. Not only will this lead to better productivity, but it will also lower your stress levels.

Time Management Guidelines

Time management skills are somewhat unique to each individual and their circumstances. What I recommend here are some generic tips that you can apply, but it's a good idea to adapt them to your unique situation.

- **Learn to say no:** People-pleasing has become a disease of our time. People are so scared about the possible negative impact on their reputation if they refuse to help others that it often leads to burnout. And in turn, people-pleasing is born from a lack of self-confidence, from a need for external validation by others. But saying no is the best way to ensure that you can focus on your primary responsibilities. I'm not saying you should never help others, but you have to prioritize your business schedule. And if you learn to say no politely and explain your reasons for doing so, you'll gain more respect than you will lose. People will respect you for being firm about your viewpoint and the boundaries that you set for undertaking other work. The business goals come first.
- **Delegate:** We covered delegation extensively already. Suffice it to say that running a business means you have to delegate. It not only saves you time and effort but ensures that the whole team feels involved in the work.

- **Keep a schedule:** It seems like an obvious thing to do but you'd be surprised how many people don't do this. With all the computerized diary aids we have now it's a simple matter. The easiest option is just a simple "To-Do" list. You can do this based on your business goals and objectives from your strategy and business plan. Every morning, look at those objectives and decide how you're going to do them today and prioritize them (we cover that next). It's also a good idea to break down your to-do list into two separate lists: work and personal.

- **Prioritize:** It's important to prioritize your tasks at the beginning of every day. Stephen Covey in his bestseller *The 7 Habits of Highly Effective People* reminds us to prioritize our tasks according to a matrix. On the one axis are important versus unimportant, and on the other urgent and not urgent. So, in quadrant 1 you'll find the tasks that are urgent and important. These cannot be postponed and must be prioritized in your to-do list. Quadrant 2 contains those things that are important but not urgent, typically longer-term strategy stuff that you can afford to postpone doing somewhat. Be careful not to postpone them too long, though, or else they don't get done! Remember they are still important. Quadrant 3 contains those tasks that are urgent and not important that you can consider delegating. And quadrant 4 contains those tasks that are neither urgent nor important. You may have to consider whether they need doing at all.

- **Develop milestones and deadlines:** Remember that

your goals and tasks have to be SMART. You have to set deadlines for every task. A task without a deadline and a responsible person behind it does not get done, believe me. If it's a significant task, perhaps part of a goal, you may have multiple deadlines, or milestones in it before it's completed. These need to be highlighted and entered into your diary, preferably an electronic one. What I do is add another date for the completion of my task about a week before the milestone or deadline, just to remind myself to start, if I haven't done so yet. As a manager, it's important to inculcate this mindset into your people, as well. There's nothing so frustrating as noticing one of your people starting on a particularly challenging assignment the day before it has to be completed.

- **Don't procrastinate:** As they say, procrastination is the thief of time. And not for no reason. Especially when we're faced with a particularly difficult or challenging task, we tend to find ways to avoid getting started. Try to break it down into small chunks so that it doesn't seem so daunting. Though, as a boss of mine used to say, "at the end of the day the only way to start is to start..."

- **Deal with your stress:** Stress impacts us at a cellular level and can result in mental and physical problems, as we covered before. Either way, it's bound to impact our productivity negatively. Stress manifests itself differently in different people. For some, it becomes an inability to focus. Others get physically ill. Others develop tremors. Yet another person may become moody and withdrawn. It all contributes to having a less engaged team. When you notice that several people in your business are becoming stressed, you have to ask yourself what your contribution as the leader is to the situation. Consider changing your management style and introduce some extracurricular activities like walking, exercising, listening to music, having a team-building session, or something similar. If there's a problem that's affecting the group, it's invariably a result of some communication problems, and I illustrated how that can be approached with team-building.

- **Don't multitask:** Many people seem to think that being able to multitask is a cool way of getting things done and that the more you can multitask the better manager you are. Maybe. In my experience, that's seldom the case though. I find I get better job satisfaction by prioritizing my work properly and getting a handle on each unique piece of work, completing it, and moving on to the next. Most people just cannot keep too many balls in the air at the same time without some quality problems slipping in.

- **Start your day early:** The one common denominator that links all high achievers together is their ability to manage time better than other mere mortals. And one of the ways they do that is by getting up two hours earlier in the mornings than others. Just think about how much more time you have to do extra work if you get up at 4 as compared to 6. If you do that consistently for five days a week, eleven months a year (accepting you take a month's leave), it gives you almost three months extra of available time in a year! That's a lot of time in which to do problem-solving for your business, get your head stuck into some marketing campaigns, or write that book!

- **Take breaks:** It's a good habit to learn, both for you and your team, to take regular breaks from work. Coffee or water cooler breaks tend to break the tension in the workspace and, if managed properly, your employees can seamlessly carry on with work without even realizing that's what they're doing by facilitating the process of relaxation to focus also on work issues at hand. This is one way of getting out of the linear thinking pattern of work always having to be done in an office or cubicle. Develop the outcomes to be achieved and let your team find their way of arriving at them. It also leads to much higher motivation and engagement.

11

WRITING THE BUSINESS PLAN

"The best business plans are straightforward documents that spell out the who, what, where, why, and how much."
—Paula Nelson

So, you might be asking, "Why does she only get to the business plan now? Surely that should have been covered in Chapter 3, at least?" Well, yes and no.

To make the book nice and tidy, the business plan should probably be toward the end of Chapter 3, just after the Financial Action Plan section. But, as I will show, everything that I covered in this book is needed for you to develop your business plan optimally. Thus, I thought it a good idea to put it at the end so that you can see the logic behind why we covered the chapters as we did.

What to Include in Your Plan

First, it's important to know that there are many different business plan formats and templates. A quick internet search will
reveal that much. But before you start with your detailed plan,
the following are important considerations:

You must have done your overall business strategy first.

You must have done a great deal of research into your
market and industry. No doubt you've done this long before
now (because you had to do that to develop the strategy and
marketing approach), but if not, now's the time to do it.

All sections of the plan are interrelated. So, although there
may not be a section on team motivation, there may very well
be a financial budget item for team building. Similarly,
although there may not be an item termed "time management,"
there may very well be a cost bucket for continuous training, in
which one of the courses may be on time management. So,
everything in this book is relevant to your business plan.

Because everything is interrelated, the person or persons
writing the plan need to be very aware of every part of the business. For that reason, it's best that you, as the leader, do it yourself. This is one of those inalienable, non-delegable tasks.

Although formats differ, a business plan will generally
consist of three parts:

- The business concept
- The marketing section
- The financial section

Remember that your business plan is normally short-term,
i.e. one year. It could indicate longer-term spending require-

ments though. The aim of writing it is to guide your actions during the next year, but it's also vitally important as a source document when you apply for funding at, for instance, a bank. They'll invariably ask you for your business plan, past financial statements, and even your strategy.

The Content

Executive Summary

This is the most important part of the document, because this is what will capture the reader's attention or make them decide to discard the document. It's always written last.

Elements to include in the executive summary include the business concept, financial features, financial requirements, major achievements, and current business position.

General Company Description

This section normally follows after the executive summary. It serves as an introduction and includes things like the name of the company, type of legal entity, ownership, significant assets, mission statement of the business, company goals and objectives, and company strengths and core competencies.

Try not to put too much detail in here, as there are many other places where you can put relevant information on marketing, finances, etc.

The Opportunity, Industry, and Market Description

- **The opportunity:** Describe why there's a gap in the market, what has given rise to it, and how it can be filled.
- **The industry:** Describe the forces impacting the industry you're planning to operate in. The general attractiveness of the industry, according to Porter's Five Forces Framework, includes considering matters like barriers to entry, customers, suppliers, substitute products, and the competition.
- **The market:** Present your insights into potential customers for your product or service by considering matters like market size, the pace at which the market is growing, market share that you intend to attract, and major trends in the market.

Strategy

Your strategy will have been developed by now, but in your business plan make sure that you include at least the following:

- What will you be offering that is different from the competition?
- How will you provide customer value?
- What will be the focus of your business; mass-market or differentiation, or both?
- How will you ensure business success?

Business Model

A good business model focuses on three things—attracting high-value customers, offering them significant value, and delivering good margins. Hence your business model should focus on highlighting costs of generating revenue, profitability, the investment required, and critical success factors for making the model work.

The Team

The business organization description should include the following:

- A list of the founders with their experience and qualifications.
- A description of who will manage the business daily, along with their experiences and competencies.
- An organization chart, showing key responsibilities and reporting lines.

Marketing Plan

The marketing plan will be drawn directly from the work that you've already done and will include matters like:

- The product or service to be provided and why it will be important for customers
- A detailed description of the target market
- The product or service positioning and branding
- The pricing strategy

- The promotion strategy, including advertising

Operational Plan

The operational plan explains how the business will function on a regular basis. The sections to be included will vary depending on the type of business, but could include matters like:

- Business operating cycle to produce the products or services
- A description of where materials and skills may be obtained
- The outsourcing relationships, if any
- The cash payments and cash receipt process of the business

Financial Plan

This is an important part if you're preparing the business plan to attract investors. Don't put too much detail into the plan. You can always include that in an appendix. Make sure that you have good visuals like graphs and maps, because that's generally what will attract an astute investor. Specific thing to consider are:

- Start-up funding requirements
- One-year profit and loss projection
- One-year cash-flow projection
- Projected balance sheet up to the end of year three
- A break-even calculation

Everything else can be included in appendices. It's generally a good idea not to make the business plan itself too bulky or too lengthy. Another reason why you need an excellent executive summary (Fisher, 2018).

It should be evident that a business plan is critical to the success of a business. It needs to be reviewed and update frequently to make sure that it keeps abreast of changes within your business environment. In this way it becomes just better and better over time. Astute business leaders use it to see how their businesses have developed historically and what lessons are to be drawn from these historical developments. The value of having a good business plan does not only relate to its use in convincing funders to support you but is also important to maximize your profits and to enhance the value of the business, should you decide to sell one day. In this way you can secure the best possible price.

CONCLUSION

This book—*Essential Small Business Leadership Skills: Develop Your Organization and Structure, Achieve Small Business Growth, and Complete Complex Business Tasks*—was all about providing you with guidelines and advice on how to run a successful small business. Right at the start, I said that this book would give you practical advice for business success and that it would highlight the skills that every entrepreneur should possess. Many such potential skills are needed, but this book focused on the most important.

Did you get all of that from the book? I sure hope so! Let's summarize what we have learned.

Chapter 1 covered the power of motivation. I deliberately started with this chapter, because I've found over the years that getting your people engaged and motivated is one of the cornerstones of running a successful business. You may have all the brightest people on board, you may have all the best-laid plans, but if your people aren't engaged, it all comes to naught.

We also showed that organizations and teams go through various stages in their development, from Forming, Storming, Norming, through to Performing. And the leader needs to be mindful of the characteristics of each stage and what he or she needs to do to nurture the team and manage them properly in each stage.

In Chapter 2, we considered the topic of emotional intelligence for leaders. We looked at what the concept means, the differences from EQ, and also how EI works in practice. I showed that having high levels of EI is important for a business leader because it allows you to show empathy to your people and assist with their motivation, and allows you to become more self-aware so that you can engage with others better.

In that chapter, we also looked at the important matter of conflict management and effective communication. Those two topics go hand-in-hand, because the reason for conflict most of the time is to be found in ineffective communication. Conversely, solving conflict is always done by promoting proper communication. Lastly, we looked at the art of delegation and why it's important. You can only get results through your people, so you had better learn how to delegate tasks effectively to them.

Chapter 3 covered financial planning. We started by explaining the concept of strategy, what it means and why it's important. Many businesses dive straight into the financial planning part of things, but if it's not based on some form of overarching, long-term strategy, you're likely to struggle because there's no central pillar around which your financial plans can be anchored.

Other important topics that we covered included business goals and objectives, the importance of financial planning, how to determine the financial status of a business, and what to do with that bit of extra that you may have left from a savings point of view.

In Chapter 4, we covered team building. We looked at what it is, the advantages, and how to go about it. This built on the initial discussion we had about team development in Chapter 1. Developing your team is an exercise in communication. It all starts and ends with establishing proper processes to promote effective communication in your business.

Building on the value of having good communication approaches, we looked at how to develop your business network in Chapter 5. Networking is an important tool to promote your business, especially if you're a small business owner. We looked at the various networking groups that you may consider joining, the importance of social media network-ing, which is all the rage nowadays, and gave some tips about how to go about doing networking. Communication skills are, again, key (isn't it interesting that the importance of having good communications skills keeps running throughout the book as a central theme?).

Chapter 6 was about critical thinking skills, what they are, the benefits of having such skills, and ways in which to improve them. There's actually a great link between this chapter and Chapter 2 on EI. Having high EI and well-developed critical thinking skills are what set a top business leader apart from the mediocre. Many people think that you either have it or you don't, but that's a fallacy. Critical thinking skills can be devel-oped, as I showed.

Chapter 7 covered the important topic of marketing. Whether you like it or not, any business is dead in the water if you don't know how to market your product or service properly.

We covered a wide range of topics, including types of marketing, the differences between marketing, sales, and advertising, and we covered the basic marketing concepts. No discussion on marketing would be complete, however, without covering the 4 Ps and the 7 Cs. We ended the chapter by providing a guideline of how to develop your marketing strategy.

In Chapter 8, we covered what many may consider a "peripheral" issue to small business leadership, namely honesty. Such a perception would, however, be erroneous. Being dishonest can destroy your reputation and put you out of business. As the leader, the buck stops with you to set an example for your people and show customers that you're honest and trustworthy to the core. We looked at some of the rewards of being honest which, apart from the intrinsic value of feeling good about yourself, will also lead to business success and a happy team working for you. Associated issues that we discussed in some detail were integrity and ethics and we showed that integrity is a wide concept, wider than honesty because it also includes how you demonstrate your honesty in practice.

Chapter 9 was about decision-making and problem-solving, a topic that I, personally, enjoy immensely because it's so varied. I covered the three basic decision-making styles and showed that we all use a combination of them, although each of us has a preference for a certain style. This, in turn, influences your approach to solving problems. There are many ways to solve problems, and the "right" way is largely determined by the context within which you find yourself. I presented the generic six-step problem-solving approach that works well to address most kinds of problems that you may encounter in business. It's a good idea to use this and experiment with the content until you've worked out a formula that will suit your needs, and those of your people, perfectly. There are many advantages to having a formal problem-solving approach in place, not least of which is that it gives you and your employees peace of mind that there's always some fallback mechanism in place to address difficult issues should they pop up.

In Chapter 10, we concluded by covering the issue of being productive with time. Not for nothing did we call it that, because productivity and proper time management go hand-in-hand. The best business leaders are those that can manage their time properly. Most of your resources are replenishable. Time is not. We gave some guidelines as to how you can go about managing your time properly.

Chapter 11 covered the basis of what is needed in a business plan. We left that to last because everything that you read in this book needs to be factored into your business plan, either directly or indirectly. There are a number of different sections in a business plan, covering amongst others aspects like the operational plan, marketing plan, and financial plan, to name only three. But we highlight the importance of the executive summary because that is where you will get the attention of your investors or lose it.

There are many small business owners out there, most of them mediocre. You don't have to be one of those. Use these guidelines that I present in this book and you can be among the best! It's all about continuous improvement, starting with yourself. People are important. Resources are important. The business idea is important. So are strategy, marketing, teambuilding, etc.

But YOU are the most important. It all starts and ends with

you. Your leadership skills and approach and your knowledge. You find that all in this book!

I do hope you enjoyed this book and now find you can use it as a reference guide for the future. I would love to hear from you and would really appreciate it if you can find the time to leave a review on Amazon!

Please use the link below to access your free business downloads.

www.smallbusinessleadershipskills.com

REFERENCES

The 7 best small business groups for networking. (n.d.). Insureon. Retrieved 2021, from https://www.insureon.com/blog/best-small-business-groups-for-networking

7 steps to create an action plan for your business strategy. (n.d.). BDC. Retrieved 2021, from https://www.bdc.ca/en/articles-tools/business-strategy-planning/define-strategy/7-steps-create-action-plan-business-strategy

8 Factors That Determine the Financial Health of a Business. (2015). Entrepreneur Media, Inc. https://www.entrepreneur.com/article/240611#:~:text=To%20get%20an%20idea%20of%20the%20company%E2%80%99s%20anticipated,are%20all%20key%20indicators%20of%20a%20business%E2%80%99s%20health.

10 Differences between a Businessman and Entrepreneur. (2019). Website Income. https://websiteincome.com/10-differences-between-a-businessman-and-entrepreneur/

Achiever. (n.d.). Cambridge Dictionary. Retrieved 2021, from https://dictionary.cambridge.org/dictionary/english/achiever

Alban, D. (n.d.). Why critical thinking is important (& how to improve it). Be Brain Fit. Retrieved 2021, from https://bebrainfit.com/critical-thinking/#:~:text=Critical%20thinking%20will%20enable%20you%20to%20better%20express,be%20applied%20to%20any%20area%20of%20your%20life.

Altman, I. (2017). 3 Ways To Make New Habits Stick. Forbes. https://www.forbes.com/sites/ianaltman/2017/08/22/3-ways-to-make-new-habits-stick/?sh=4ec96535378a

The Art of Effective Delegation. (n.d.). Free Management Books. Retrieved 2021, from http://www.free-management-ebooks.com/news/the-art-of-effective-delega-tion/#:~:text=%20The%20Art%20of%20Effective%20Delegation%20%201,taken%20literally%20when%20it%20comes%20to..%20More%20

Balanced Scorecard Basics. (n.d.). Balanced Scorecard Institute. Retrieved 2021, from https://balancedscorecard.org/bsc-basics-overview/

Belyh, A. (2020). Exciting 13 Successful People's Everyday Tricks to Your Life Goals. Cleverism. https://www.cleverism.com/emulating-13-successful-peoples-everyday-tricks-to-your-life-goals/

Blaikie, R. (2019). *Design and Develop Effective Teams [Slides]. Udemy.* https://www.udemy.com/course/design-and-develop-effective-teams/learn/lecture/7013736#overview

Boitnott, J. (2017). *10 Ways You Should Invest Your Company's First Profits. Entrepreneur Media, Inc.* https://www.entrepreneur.com/article/288456

Brinson, L. (n.d.). *How Business Networking Works. Hostuffworks.* Retrieved 2021, from https://money.howstuffworks.com/business/professional-development/business-networking.htm

Brown, H. (2021). *What is Emotional Intelligence? +23 Ways To Improve It. Positive Psychology.* https://positivepsychology.com/emotional-intelligence-eq/

Clapon, P. (2017). *Extracting Talent: How to Unlock the Full Potential of Each of Your Employees. The HR & Employee Engagement Community.* https://gethppy.com/talent-management/extracting-talent-unlock-full-potential-employees

Corporate Strategy Board. (1999). *Proceedings in Daylight: Frontier Practices in Challenging Strategic Assumptions. Washington D.C: Corporate Executive Board.*

Critical thinking. (n.d.). *Wikipedia.* https://en.wikipedia.org/wiki/Critical_thinking

Cutruzzula, K. (2020). *7 Ways to Regain Your Footing (and Self-Worth) After You Disappoint Yourself. Shine.* https://advice.theshineapp.com/articles/7-ways-to-regain-your-footing-and-self-worth-after-you-disappoint-yourself/

de Flander, J. (2019). *The Art of Performance (1st ed.).* The Performance Factory.

Develop a marketing strategy. (2021). *Business Queensland.* https://www.business.qld.gov.au/running-business/marketing-sales/marketing-promotion/strategy

Difference Between Ethics and Integrity. (2015). Difference Between.Com. https://www.differencebetween.com/difference-between-ethics-and-vs-integrity/

Emotional Intelligence in Leadership. (n.d.). Mind Tools. Retrieved 2021, from https://www.mindtools.com/pages/article/newLDR_45.htm

Engage Your Employees to See High Performance and Innovation. (2021). Gallup. https://www.gallup.com/workplace/229424/employee-engagement.aspx

Financial Planning. (2020). Toppr. https://www.toppr.com/guides/business-studies/financial-management/financial-planning/#:~:text=Financial%20planning%20is%20the%20plan%20needed%20for%20estimating,generally%20includes%20long-term%20investment%2C%20growth%20and%20financing%20decisions.

Fisher, G. (2018). *Business Plan Format Guide. ExpertHub.* *https://www.experthub.info/launch/business-plans/business-plan-format/business-plan-format-guide/*

Forming, Storming, Norming, and Performing. Tuckman's Model for Nurturing a Team to High Performance. (2020). *Mind Tools.* *https://www.mindtools.com/pages/article/newLDR_86.htm*

Forsey, C. (2021). *What is Marketing, and What's Its Purpose?* *HubSpot. https://blog.hubspot.com/marketing/what-is-marketing*

Golis, C. (2021). *How to Increase your EQ: The 7MTF Model of Temperament. Practical Emotional Intelligence. https://www.emotionalintelligencecourse.com/increase-your-eq/*

Hart, M. (2019). *What's the Difference Between Sales and Marketing? A Simple & Easy Primer. HubSpot. https://blog.hubspot.com/sales/sales-and-marketing*

Hassell, D. (n.d.). *Your Employees are Planning to Jump Ship. 15Five. Retrieved 2021, from https://www.15five.com/blog/employee-engagement-the-key-to-unlocking-your-teams-potential/*

Hasyap, S. (n.d.). *Here's How Effective Communication is in the Hands of 73% of Professionals. ProofHub. Retrieved 2021, from https://www.proofhub.com/articles/effective-communication*

Hatch, C. (2020). *5 Essential Marketing Concepts You Should Know. Disruptive. https://disruptiveadvertising.com/marketing/marketing-concepts/*

HubSpot. (2021). Not Another State of Marketing Report. CXD Studio. https://www.hubspot.com/state-of-marketing

Keys to Healthier Mind Development. (2021). Emotional Intelligence Institute. https://e-ii.org/learn-what-ei-and-eq-mean/

Kim, W., & Mauborgne, R. (2015). Blue Ocean Strategy - Expanded Edition. Harvard Business Review Press.

Kraus, D. (2019). Unlock the potential of your team: How to develop winning minds. Smart Company. https://www.smartcompany.-com.au/partner-content/articles/unlock-the-potential-of-your-team/

Kukreja, R. (2021). 10 Practical Ways to Improve Time Management Skills. Lifehack. https://www.lifehack.org/articles/productivity/10-ways-improve-your-time-management-skills.html

Landau, P. (2019). 30 Best Business Quotes to Inspire Entrepreneurs & Go-Getters. ProjectManager.Com. https://www.projectmanager.-com/blog/30-best-business-quotes

Leaf, C. (2021). Cleaning Up Your Mental Mess (1st ed.). Baker Books.

Loewen, J. (1997). The Power of Strategy A Practical Guide for South African Managers. Zebra Press.

Manthei, L. (2017). The 4 Ps of Marketing: Understanding the Marketing Mix. Emarsys. https://emarsys.com/learn/blog/4-ps-of-marketing-importance/

Martins, A. (n.d.). *How to Write a Business Plan Goals & Objectives.* *Profitable Venture Magazine Ltd.* Retrieved 2021, from *https://www.profitableventure.com/business-plan-goals-objectives/*

Oberoi, A. (2020). *9 Practical Ways to Discipline Yourself Quickly.* *Kool Stories.* *https://www.koolstories.com/blog/practical-ways-to-discipline-yourself*

Onley, D. (2019). *How Leaders Can Make Better Decisions. SHRM.* *https://www.shrm.org/hr-today/news/hr-magazine/fall2019/pages/how-leaders-can-make-better-decisions.aspx*

Pfeiffer, J. (1985). *Understanding Applied Strategic Planning: A Manager's Guide. University Associates, Inc.*

Prachi. (2018). *Team Building. The Investors Book.* *https://theinvestorsbook.com/team-building.html*

Process of Team Building. (n.d.). *MBA Knowledge Base.* Retrieved 2021, from *https://www.mbaknol.com/management-principles/process-of-team-building/*

Reilly, R. (2021). *5 Ways to Improve Employee Engagement Now.* *Gallup.* *https://www.gallup.com/workplace/231581/five-ways-improve-employee-engagement.aspx*

Roy, E. (2017). *The Seven C's You Need to Organize Your Marketing Strategy. Trade Ready.* *https://www.tradeready.ca/2017/topics/marketingsales/seven-cs-need-organize-marketing-strategy/*

Scuderi, R. (n.d.). *How To Handle Personality Conflicts At Work.* Lifehack. Retrieved 2021, from https://www.lifehack.org/articles/communication/how-to-handle-personality-conflicts-at-work.html

Silva, L. (2017). *THE REAL BENEFITS OF HONESTY IN THE WORKPLACE.* Influencive. https://www.influencive.com/real-benefits-honesty-workplace/#:~:text=A%20reputation%20for%20honesty%20is%20the%20kind%20of,that%20hurdle%2C%20it%20can%20also%20be%20tremendously%20rewarding.

The Six Step Problem Solving Model. (n.d.). Free Management Books. Retrieved 2021, from http://www.free-management-ebooks.com/news/six-step-problem-solving-model/

Soh, R. (2017). *10 Benefits of Self-Discipline.* Seek Five. https://seek-five.org/10-benefits-of-self-discipline/

Strategy is the direction and scope of an organisation. (2008). UKEssays. https://www.ukessays.com/essays/business/strategy-is-the-direction-and-scope-of-an-organisation-business-essay.php

Thomas, J. (n.d.). *Honesty Is Not Synonymous With Integrity, And We Need To Know The Difference, For Integrity Is What We Need.* Alliance for Integrity. Retrieved 2021, from http://allianceforintegrity.com/integrity-articles/honesty-is-not-synonymous-with-integrityand-we-need-to-know-the-differencefor-integrity-is-what-we-need/#sthash.vqxBdNvS.dpbs

Tracy, B. (2017). *The Importance Of Honesty And Integrity In Business.* Entrepreneur. https://www.entrepreneur.com/article/282957

What is the Role of a Financial Planner? (n.d.). Ignite Financial Planning. Retrieved 2021, from https://www.ignitefinancialplanning.-com/post/what-is-the-role-of-a-financial-planner

Wheeler, D., & Bhadresa, S. (2020). Four ways to empower teams and unlock potential. Personnel Today. https://www.personneltoday.-com/hr/how-to-empower-teams/

Wilson, M. (2020). THE FIVE MARKETING CONCEPTS. Avalaunch Media. https://avalaunchmedia.com/the-five-marketing-concepts/

Young, S. (n.d.). 18 Tricks to Make New Habits Stick. Lifehack. Retrieved 2021, from https://www.lifehack.org/articles/featured/18-tricks-to-make-new-habits-stick.html

THANK YOU

Thank you so much for reading this book. I would love it if you could spare a few minutes of your time to review my book on amazon. It is really important to me to get your feedback and let others know that this book can help them on their journey.

FREE DOWNLOAD

Please follow the link below to register for our free business downloads:
www.smallbusinessleadershipskills.com

ABOUT THE AUTHOR

About the Author

Hi. My name is Diana Armstrong and I'm a successful business leader.

I have owned and run a small and successful business for 20 years and have worked alongside many businesses that have failed through difficult times. I often reflect on why some businesses fail and some succeed. And, in my experience, most businesses that fail do so because they don't give sufficient attention to all or some of the topics that I cover in this book.

So, I wanted to write this book to get some of the basics across, but I don't want it to be just another business leadership book. This is all about how small businesses succeed and how entrepreneurs need to be flexible and adaptable in addition to requiring key management skills. And the issue of entrepreneurship is vital in the small business world, so I give that some attention in this book.

Ultimately, this book is about leadership skills in business. For that reason, I place a great deal of emphasis on the qualities that you as the leader of the business should possess. Your people will look up to you for leadership and guidance. It's up to you to show them that leadership.

Are you ready to become a successful business person? A successful entrepreneur? Then stick with me...

f